# zoom
## Deutsch 2

# Higher Workbook

Oliver Gray

OxBox

**OXFORD**

Great Clarendon Street, Oxford OX2 6DP

Oxford University Press is a department of the University of Oxford.

It furthers the University's objective of excellence in research, scholarship,
and education by publishing worldwide in
Oxford   New York   Auckland   Cape Town   Dar es Salaam   Hong Kong   Karachi
Kuala Lumpur   Madrid   Melbourne   Mexico City   Nairobi   New Delhi   Shanghai
Taipei   Toronto

With offices in
Argentina   Austria   Brazil   Chile   Czech Republic   France   Greece   Guatemala
Hungary   Italy   Japan   South Korea   Poland   Portugal   Singapore   Switzerland
Thailand   Turkey   Ukraine   Vietnam

Oxford is a registered trade mark of Oxford University Press in the UK and in certain
other countries

British Library Cataloguing in Publication Data

Data available

ISBN 978 019 912780 1

20

Printed in India by Multivista Global Pvt. Ltd.

Paper used in the production of this book is a natural, recyclable product made
from wood grown in sustainable forests. The manufacturing process conforms to the
environmental regulations of the country of origin.

**Acknowledgements**
The author and publisher would like to thank the following people for their help and
advice: Jenny Gwynne (editor), Angelika Libera (language consultant).

Audio recordings by Colette Thomson for Footstep Productions; Andrew Garratt (engineer)

The author and publisher would like to thank the following for their permission to
reproduce photographs and other copyright material:
**p.12**: Photodisc/OUP; **p.44**: Ingo Wagner/dpa/Corbis; **p.57**: elxeneize/iStock;
**p.60**: Jo Chambers/Shutterstock; Jo Chambers/Alamy

Illustrations by: TK. Matt Ward

Every effort has been made to contact copyright holders of material reproduced in this
book. If notified, the publishers will be pleased to rectify any errors or omissions at the
earliest opportunity.

# Inhalt

**Pronunciation**    4

**Einheit 0: Hallo!**

| | | |
|---|---|---|
| 0.1 | Wie siehst du aus? | 8 |
| 0.2 | Wie bist du? | 9 |
| 0.3 | Zu Hause | 10 |
| 0.4 | Warum bist du in Köln? | 11 |
| 0.5 | Familienleben | 12 |
| 0.6A | Sprachlabor | 13 |
| 0.6B | Think | 14 |
| 0 | Vokabular | 15 |

**Einheit 1A: Mein Tag**

| | | |
|---|---|---|
| 1A.1 | Mein Alltag | 16 |
| 1A.2 | Was hast du gemacht? | 17 |
| 1A.3 | Und gestern Abend ...? | 18 |
| 1A.4 | Es war super! | 19 |
| 1A.5 | Letztes Wochenende | 20 |
| 1A.6A | Sprachlabor | 21 |
| 1A.6B | Think | 22 |
| 1A | Vokabular | 23 |

**Einheit 1B: Wir feiern!**

| | | |
|---|---|---|
| 1B.1 | Feiertage und Feste | 24 |
| 1B.2 | Party machen | 25 |
| 1B.3 | Nichts als Ausreden | 26 |
| 1B.4 | Die Party war spitze! | 27 |
| 1B.5 | Alle Jahre wieder | 28 |
| 1B.6A | Sprachlabor | 29 |
| 1B.6B | Think | 30 |
| 1B | Vokabular | 31 |

**Einheit 2A: Die Medien**

| | | |
|---|---|---|
| 2A.1 | Im Fernsehen | 32 |
| 2A.2 | Neue Medien, alte Medien | 33 |
| 2A.3 | Techno ist toll! | 34 |
| 2A.4 | Wie war der Film? | 35 |
| 2A.5 | Ich bin eine Leseratte! | 36 |
| 2A.6A | Sprachlabor | 37 |
| 2A.6B | Think | 38 |
| 2A | Vokabular | 39 |

**Einheit 2B: Hobbys**

| | | |
|---|---|---|
| 2B.1 | Mein Lieblingshobby | 40 |
| 2B.2 | Das ist ein tolles Hobby! | 41 |
| 2B.3 | Wenn es heiß ist, … | 42 |
| 2B.4 | Nächstes Wochenende | 43 |
| 2B.5 | Ungewöhnliche Hobbys! | 44 |
| 2B.6A | Sprachlabor | 45 |
| 2B.6B | Think | 46 |
| 2B | Vokabular | 47 |

**Einheit 3A: Gesundes Leben**

| | | |
|---|---|---|
| 3A.1 | Der Körper | 48 |
| 3A.2 | Was fehlt dir? | 49 |
| 3A.3 | Topfit! | 50 |
| 3A.4 | Du bist, was du isst! | 51 |
| 3A.5 | Isst du gesund? | 52 |
| 3A.6A | Sprachlabor | 53 |
| 3A.6B | Think | 54 |
| 3A | Vokabular | 55 |

**Einheit 3B: Ausflug nach Düsseldorf**

| | | |
|---|---|---|
| 3B.1 | Wir brauchen Infos! | 56 |
| 3B.2 | Was kann man machen? | 57 |
| 3B.3 | Zwei Fahrkarten, bitte! | 58 |
| 3B.4 | Wieder zu Hause! | 59 |
| 3B.5 | Eine Stadtrundfahrt | 60 |
| 3B.6A | Sprachlabor | 61 |
| 3B.6B | Think | 62 |
| 3B | Vokabular | 63 |

**Einheit 4A: Die Umwelt**

| | | |
|---|---|---|
| 4A.1 | Meine Gegend | 64 |
| 4A.2 | Bus und Bahn | 65 |
| 4A.3 | Umweltschutz | 66 |
| 4A.4 | Fünf vor zwölf | 67 |
| 4A.5 | Initiative „Grüne Schule" | 68 |
| 4A.6A | Sprachlabor | 69 |
| 4A.6B | Think | 70 |
| 4A | Vokabular | 71 |

**Einheit 4B: Schule und Zukunft**

| | | |
|---|---|---|
| 4B.1 | Ich habe einen Nebenjob | 72 |
| 4B.2 | Meine Schule | 73 |
| 4B.3 | Und nächstes Jahr? | 74 |
| 4B.4 | Berufe | 75 |
| 4B.5 | Mein Schultag | 76 |
| 4B.6A | Sprachlabor | 77 |
| 4B.6B | Think | 78 |
| 4B | Vokabular | 79 |

**CD Track listings**    80

# Pronunciation

As you listen to the recordings for pages 4–7, repeat each word or phrase; imitate the pronunciation as closely as you can, to help you sound more German.

## Consonants / Konsonanten

Many German consonants are pronounced the same way as in English. Listen to these examples.

**b** **B**erlin
**d** **D**ialog
**f** **F**isch
**h** **H**aus
**k** **K**omödie
**l** **l**ustig
**m** **M**usical
**n** **n**ein
**p** **P**olen
**t** **T**ischtennis

Fischer Fritz frisst frische Fische!

**g** Remember: *g* is always 'hard' as in 'ground', 'gap'. One exception is the 'soft g' at the end of a word imported from French: *Garage*.

 **g**

Das **G**ras ist **g**rün.
**G**ert spielt **g**ern **G**itarre.
Mor**g**en **g**ehen wir in den **G**arten.

**j** *j* is pronounced like the English '*y*'.

 **j**

Bist du in **J**apan? **J**a!
**J**etzt esse ich **J**oghurt.

**r** *r* is quite a distinctive sound in German and needs practising because no sound in English is quite like it.

 **r**

**R**üdesheim liegt am **R**hein.
**R**egen, **R**egen, immer **R**egen.
**B**ring mir einen K**r**imi.

**s** *s* is pronounced in various ways:
1 – like an English 'z'
2 – like the English 'sh'
3 – like an English 's'.

 **s**

**s**ieben

 **sp st**

Wir **s**pielen Golf.
Der Lehrer ist **s**treng.

 **s**

Wa**s** ist da**s**?
Du bi**s**t lustig.

**1** Listen to these words. What kind of s sound is there in each one? Label them 1, 2 or 3 to match the groups above.

 **s**

| | | | |
|---|---|---|---|
| **S**turm | ☐ | **s**ingen | ☐ |
| **S**ommer | ☐ | Ma**s**ke | ☐ |
| **S**kateboard | ☐ | **S**axofon | ☐ |
| **s**treng | ☐ | fa**s**t | ☐ |

**ß** *ß* represents a double *s* when used after a <u>long</u> vowel.

Regen, Regen, immer Regen.

 **ß**

Diese Stra**ß**e ist gro**ß**.
Wir lieben Fu**ß**ball.

# Pronunciation

 After a <u>short</u> vowel, *ss* is written instead. It sounds the same as *ß*.

 **ss**

Ich mu**ss** Schlu**ss** machen.
La**ss**t uns zum Schlo**ss** gehen.
Das ha**ss**e ich.

**2** Try pronouncing these words correctly, then listen to check:

 **ss**

| küssen | blass | Bassgitarre |
|--------|-------|-------------|
| Spaß | Fuß | |

 *v* is pronounced like the English 'f'.

 **v**

Es gibt so **v**iel **V**erkehr.
Sebastian **V**ettel ist Rennfahrer.
Das ist **v**öllig **v**erboten.

 *w* is pronounced like the English 'v'.

 **w**

Die Um**w**elt ist **w**ichtig.
**W**illst du **W**asserski fahren?
**W**er **w**ohnt in dieser **W**ohnung?
**W**ir **w**ollen keine **W**olken sehen.

**3** Try saying these sentences which contain *v* and *w*, and listen to check:

 **vw**

Mein **V**ater hat einen **V**olks**w**agen.
Bremerha**v**en ist nicht **w**eit von **W**ilhelmsha**v**en.

 In German, *z* is very common. It is pronounced like the English 'ts'.

 **z**

Die **Z**eit ist eine **Z**eitung.
In **Z**ürich gibt es einen **Z**oo.

## Combinations of consonants

 The combination of *c* and *h* sounds similar to the *ch* at the end of the Scottish exclamation 'och!'

 **ch**

A**ch**tung!
Bist du schon a**ch**tzehn?
La**ch**en ist gesund.
Ein Lo**ch** ist im Eimer.
Das ist e**ch**t super.

 The same *ch* sound can also come at the end of a word ending in -*ig*:

 **ig**

Du bist lust**ig**!
Heute ist es wolk**ig**.

 The *sh* sound is common in German and is spelt *sch*.

 **sch**

Engli**sch** ist **sch**wierig aber
Deut**sch** ist **sch**wieriger, sagt der
**sch**lechte **Sch**üler!

 Another common combination of consonants is *pf*:

**pf**

Ein **Pf**und **Pf**laumen, bitte.
Walter Tell hatte einen A**pf**el auf dem Ko**pf**.

Finally, *zw*. Two sounds, like English 'ts' and 'v', are put together:

**zw**

**Zw**ei ist **zw**ischen eins und drei.
Das Museum ist von **zw**ölf bis **zw**anzig Uhr geöffnet.

Lachen ist gesund.

VW

# Pronunciation

## Vowels / Vokale

 *a* can be pronounced as a long vowel or a short vowel.

🎧 **long a / langes a**

Mein V**a**ter ist auf der Str**a**ße.
Wir b**a**den jeden T**a**g.
M**a**len bringt Sp**a**ß.

🎧 **short a / kurzes a**

L**a**sst uns für F**a**sching einen Kuchen b**a**cken.
W**a**s m**a**cht der M**a**nn?
Es ist f**a**st **a**cht.

In English, *a* is a very open sound, as in the English word 'cat'. In German, *a* is almost like an English *u*, as in the English 'cut'. Listen to these words to hear the difference.

🎧

English: h**a**t      English: c**a**t
German: h**a**t      German: K**a**tze

However, when German adapts an English word, the *a* sounds more like an English *e*.

🎧 H**a**ndy

 In German, the short *e* is pronounced like the English *e* in 'elephant'. It is never pronounced like the other English *e* as in 'me'.

🎧 **short e / kurzes e**

T**e**nnis ist h**e**ktisch.
Fr**e**ddie ist fr**e**ch.
**E**ngland ist ein n**e**ttes Land.

There is also a long **e**, as underlined here:

🎧 **long e / langes e**

<u>E</u>va hat einen <u>E</u>sel.
Ich habe noch nie in meinem
L<u>e</u>ben einen <u>E</u>lefanten ges<u>e</u>hen.

---

4   Listen to these words. What kind of *e* sound is there? Write S for short, L for long.

🎧 e

| | | | |
|---|---|---|---|
| W**e**sten | ☐ | d**e**n | ☐ |
| g**e**hen | ☐ | d**e**nn | ☐ |
| T**e**st | ☐ | w**e**nn | ☐ |
| kl**e**ben | ☐ | W**e**h | ☐ |

 *i* is always pronounced short, as in the English 'in'.

🎧 i

Ich finde S**i**lvester toll.
Ich b**i**n **i**n einem Internetcafé.
K**i**nder s**i**nd n**i**cht b**i**llig.

 *o* can be short or long. The short *o* is pronounced like this:

🎧 **short o / kurzes o**

Mein C**o**mputer ist t**o**ll.
**O**liver mag **O**liven.
Ich esse **o**ft P**o**mmes.

The long *o* is pronounced like this:

🎧 **long o / langes o**

**O**stermontag
B**o**chum ist eine Großstadt.
Wir w**o**hnen an der D**o**nau.

5   Listen: what kind of *o* sound does each word have? Write S for short, L for long.

🎧

| | | | |
|---|---|---|---|
| H**o**se | ☐ | Kr**o**nberg | ☐ |
| B**o**ss | ☐ | **O**pa | ☐ |
| v**o**ll | ☐ | B**o**nn | ☐ |
| D**o**se | ☐ | | |

# Pronunciation

 *u* can be short or long. The short *u* is pronounced like this:

>  **short u / kurzes u**
>
> **U**nsere **U**mwelt m**u**ss nicht schm**u**tzig sein.
> **U**schi ist l**u**stig.

The long *u* is pronounced like this:

> **long u / langes u**
>
> Wir machen M**u**sik in der Sch**u**le.
> Hast d**u** mein B**u**ch?
> Mein H**u**t, der hat drei Ecken.

**6** Listen: what kind of *u* sound does each word have? Write S for short, L for long.

| | | | |
|---|---|---|---|
| Z**u**g | ☐ | F**u**ß | ☐ |
| m**u**tig | ☐ | t**u**t | ☐ |
| **u**nfreundlich | ☐ | K**u**ss | ☐ |

## Combinations of vowels

 *ie* is pronounced as in the English word 'keep'.

> **ie**
>
> Trink nicht zu v**ie**l B**ie**r.
> Ich l**ie**be T**ie**re.
> Wir v**ie**r sind h**ie**r.

 *ei* is pronounced as in the English word 'eye'.

> **ei**
>
> Wie h**ei**ßt du?
> M**ei**n Name ist H**ei**di.
> M**ei**ne Stadt ist k**ei**ne Kl**ei**nstadt.

**7** Read these words out loud, then listen to check:

> **ie / ei**
>
> viel       Siemens    Ziel
> dein       Bein       Biene
> Brief      seit

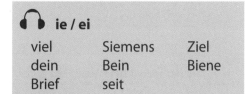 *au* is pronounced as in the English word 'cow'.

> **au**
>
> Ich mache H**au**s**au**fgaben zu H**au**se – natürlich!
> Meine bl**au**e Hose ist s**au**ber.

## Umlauts

An umlaut is a little symbol that changes the sound of an *a*, *o* or *u*. Listen to the difference the umlaut makes.

> **a ⟶ ä**
>
> Vater / Väter      Hand / Hände
> hatte / hätte      fahre / fährt

> **o ⟶ ö**
>
> Post / hören       Gott / Möwe
> rot / Löwe

Ich liebe Tiere.

> **u ⟶ ü**
>
> muss / müssen      musste / Küste
> Gruß / grüßen      fünfundfünfzig
> pur / Tür

**8** Listen to ten words. Can you identify which ones contain an umlaut? Here are the main vowels in these words: add an umlaut if you think it is necessary.

> | | | | | |
> |---|---|---|---|---|
> | 1 **u** | 2 **u** | 3 **u** | 4 **u** | 5 **o** |
> | 6 **o** | 7 **a** | 8 **a** | 9 **u** | 10 **u** |

# 0.1  Wie siehst du aus?

**1**  **Read about these two people. Draw pictures to show what they look like.**

> Meine Freundin Vanessa sieht anders aus als Peter. Sie hat braune Augen und lange braune lockige Haare. Sie trägt keine Brille, aber manchmal trägt sie Ohrringe, meistens wenn sie zu Partys geht. Ich finde Vanessa ganz toll!

Vanessa

> Mein Freund Peter ist sehr cool. Er hat blaue Augen und er trägt eine Brille. Er trägt auch einen Ohrring. Er hat kurze glatte Haare.

Peter

**2**  🎧 **Listen to this girl describing herself. Answer the questions in English.**

**a**  What colour is Sylvia's hair?  _____blonde_____

**b**  What does she say about the length of her hair?  _____

**c**  Is it straight?  _____

**d**  What colour eyes does she have?  _____

**e**  What two other things do we find out about her?  _____

**3**  **Choose one girl and one boy in your class. Write a brief description of each (hair, eyes, etc). Pass your description to a partner. Can your partner work out who you are describing?**

_____

_____

_____

_____

_____

_____

**1** Find ten words describing character in this wordsearch. They can be across, down or diagonal.

| A | I | ß | C | Ö | F | P | C | I | G | O | H |
|---|---|---|---|---|---|---|---|---|---|---|---|
| W | S | Y | M | P | A | T | H | I | S | C | H |
| B | K | A | H | N | T | U | H | L | I | O | S |
| S | E | G | Ü | E | Ö | B | Ü | L | K | D | C |
| H | A | M | N | N | L | R | D | U | B | Z | H |
| P | R | W | D | Z | A | N | Z | S | C | S | Ü |
| ß | R | G | Ö | J | U | N | A | T | M | F | C |
| B | O | Ü | F | E | N | E | K | I | E | ß | H |
| W | G | I | R | Ö | I | R | F | G | A | J | T |
| M | A | F | E | A | S | V | Z | D | E | R | E |
| N | N | L | C | U | C | I | E | J | Z | F | R |
| U | T | G | H | B | H | G | E | M | E | I | N |

**2** 🎧 Listen to six comments about people. Write the opinion words in English. Two comments also give reasons for their opinions: note these down too.

1   moody _____

2   _____

3   _____

4   _____

5   _____

6   _____

**3** Provide the second half of each sentence, in German, following the cues in brackets.

**a** Ich mag Mehmet, _____ .

   (*because he's friendly*)

**b** Ich mag Yesim nicht, _____ .

   (*because she's mean*)

**c** Ich mag Doris, _____ .

   (*because she's nice*)

**1** **Draw lines to link the pictures to the matching sentences.**

1

2

3

4

5

6

**a** Ich kaufe oft im Supermarkt ein.

**b** Ich wasche nie ab.

**c** Manchmal füttere ich die Katze.

**d** Ich decke manchmal den Tisch.

**e** Ich räume mein Zimmer jeden Tag auf.

**f** Ich sauge Staub am Wochenende.

**2** **Choose a German adjective to describe each of these people.**

**a** A dad who plays music from his youth.          *altmodisch*

**b** A mum who won't let her child play outside.          _____

**c** A parent who gets annoyed if someone is late.          _____

**d** Parents who have cool phones.          _____

**e** A mum who doesn't mind if her children are out late.          _____

**3** 🎧 **Listen: which of the parents in Activity 2 is being described?**

1 __d__          2 _____          3 _____

4 _____          5 _____

**1**   **Read these sentences. After each, write whether it is <u>present</u> or <u>perfect</u> tense.**

**a**   Ich bin oft nach Dortmund gefahren.      _perfect_

**b**   Hassan hat im Internet einen Blog geschrieben.     _____

**c**   Lara schreibt einen Blog über ihre Haustiere.     _____

**d**   Hast du schon ein Handy gekauft?     _____

**e**   Ben tanzt gern auf Partys.     _____

**f**   Was machst du im Moment?     _____

**g**   Ich kaufe oft Bonbons, aber sie sind nicht gut!     _____

**h**   Ich habe ein Interview bei Radio Zoom gemacht.     _____

**2**   🎧 **Listen to someone talking about a day out. Write down the seven things he does, in English, in the correct order. Add details if you can.**

_Walked into town (Saturday)_

_____

_____

_____

_____

_____

_____

**3**   **Choose an appropriate German past participle to add to each sentence.**

**a**   Ich habe für meine Schwester eine neuen Computer _gekauft_ .

**b**   Er ist nach der Schule zu Fuß nach Hause _____ .

**c**   Ich habe ein neues Buch über Autos _____ .

**d**   Sie hat einen Brief an ihre Schwester _____ .

**e**   Du bist mit dem Zug nach Nienburg _____ .

**f**   Im China-Restaurant haben wir Nudeln _____ .

# 0.5 Familienleben

**1** Look at these mixed-up words. Each one could be used to describe someone's character. Write them out correctly and provide the English translation.

a **rcnflduieh** _____freundlich_____ _____friendly_____

b **retnsg** _____ _____

c **uelnduigdg** _____ _____

d **rotnaarg** _____ _____

e **scilprtoh** _____ _____

f **megine** _____ _____

**2** 🎧 Listen to Samira. What did she do yesterday? Put a tick or a cross by each sentence.

a She fed the dog. ☒

b She cleaned her bike. ☐

c She washed up. ☐

d She stayed in bed. ☐

e She did her maths homework. ☐

f She went into town. ☐

g She cleaned the bathroom. ☐

h She tidied her bedroom. ☐

**3** Translate these sentences into German, using the perfect tense.

a We bought a car. _Wir haben ..._____

b I drove to Berlin. _____

c I cleared up the bathroom. _____

d We went to the disco. _____

e I ate spaghetti. _____

> **Remember:**
> *fahren* and *gehen* use *sein* to form the perfect tense.

**1** **Put a tick by all the sentences which have the correct word order. Cross out those that don't.**

a Herr Meyer ist streng, aber er auch nett ist. ☐

b Ich mag Lars, weil er ist lustig. ☐

c Ich mag Claudia nicht, weil sie arrogant ist. ☐

d Ich putze das Badezimmer und ich räume auf. ☐

e Ich mag Ulla, weil sie hat blonde Haare. ☐

f Wir haben Pizza gemacht, weil wir Hunger haben. ☐

> *weil* (because) is a linking word which changes the word order. It sends the verb to the end:
> Ich mag Sira. Sie **ist** lustig.
> → Ich mag Sira, **weil** sie lustig **ist**.
>
> Other linking words such as *und* and *aber* don't change the word order:
> Ich mag Sira und sie ist lustig.

**2** **Write out the three crossed-out sentences correctly.**

_____

_____

_____

**3** **Make up three new sentences of your choice, using *weil*.**

_____

_____

_____

**4** **Fill the gaps with part of *haben* or *sein* and the past participle.**

a Ich ___habe___ eine CD ___gekauft___ . (*bought*)

b Wir _____ ins Restaurant _____ . (*went*)

c Du _____ eine E-Mail _____ . (*wrote*)

d Hassan _____ Fußball _____ . (*played*)

e Wir _____ nach Spanien _____ . (*travelled*)

f Ich _____ das Praktikum _____ . (*got*)

> **The perfect tense with *haben* and *sein***
> Most verbs form their perfect tense with *haben*, and their past participles start with *ge-* and end with *-t*: Ich **habe** Fußball **ge**spiel**t**.
>
> A few verbs (mostly verbs of movement) use *sein* instead of *haben* to form the perfect tense. Most of their past participles start with *ge-* but end with *-en*: Ich **bin** in die Disco **ge**gang**en**.

**5** **Choose three sentences from Activity 4 to translate into English.**

_____

_____

_____

**die Super-Jungs**

Die Super-Jungs sind eine neue Boygroup aus Krefeld. Ihre Fans finden sie toll, aber wie sind die Super-Jungs wirklich? Wir haben sie gefragt.

Marek

Kai

**Kai:**
Ich tanze gut und ich singe auch gut. Einige Fans finden mich arrogant. Naja, okay, ich bin ein bisschen arrogant, aber ich bin auch sehr freundlich.

Omar

Phillipp

**Marek:**
Ich bin absolut nicht arrogant! Alle Mädchen mögen mich, weil ich schöne Haare und braune Augen habe. Ich bin manchmal launisch, aber nie gemein.

**Omar:**
Ich habe lockige Haare und trage einen Ohrring. Die Mädchen sagen, ich bin der Beste in der Band, weil ich so nett und auch sympathisch bin.

**Phillipp:**
Ich bin schüchtern, aber manchmal auch ein bisschen frech. Ich bin beliebt, weil ich nie unfreundlich bin.

**_1_ Read the magazine article and answer the questions below.**

**a** Underline all the adjectives in the interview.

**b** Double underline all the adjectives which come before a noun and therefore have an ending.

**c** Find one adjective exactly the same as in English and three that are similar to English.

The same: _____

Similar: _____  _____  _____

**d** Which adjectives, in your opinion, are difficult to guess because they are completely unlike English words?

_____

**e** Have an intelligent guess at what *beliebt* means. _____

**f** What could *einige* mean? _____

**g** Why is *sympathisch* a false friend?

_____

## Wie siehst du aus? — *What do you look like?*

| | |
|---|---|
| Wie sieht er/sie aus? | *What does he/she look like?* |
| Ich habe/Er hat/Sie hat … | *I have/He has/She has …* |
|   blaue/braune/grüne Augen. | *blue/brown/green eyes.* |
|   blonde/braune/rote/ schwarze Haare. | *blonde/brown/red/black hair.* |
|   lange/kurze/lockige/ glatte Haare. | *long/short/curly/straight hair.* |
| Trägst du …? Trägt er/sie …? | *Do you wear …? Does he/she wear …?* |
| Ich trage/Er trägt/Sie trägt … | *I wear/He wears/She wears …* |
|   eine Brille/einen Ohrring. | *glasses/an earring.* |
| Ich trage keine Brille/keinen Ohrring. | *I don't wear glasses/an earring.* |

## Wie bist du? — *What's your character like?*

| | |
|---|---|
| Ich bin/Er ist/Sie ist … | *I am/He is/She is …* |
| arrogant | *arrogant* |
| frech | *naughty* |
| freundlich | *friendly* |
| gemein | *mean* |
| launisch | *moody* |
| lustig | *funny* |
| nervig | *irritating* |
| nett | *nice* |
| schüchtern | *shy* |
| sympathisch | *nice* |
| unfreundlich | *unfriendly* |
| | |
| immer | *always* |
| manchmal | *sometimes* |
| nicht | *not* |
| nie | *never* |
| oft | *often* |
| sehr | *very* |
| selten | *rarely, seldom* |
| ziemlich | *quite* |
| Ich mag …, weil er/sie (nicht) … ist. | *I like … because he/she is (isn't) …* |

## Zu Hause — *At home*

| | |
|---|---|
| Meine Eltern sind … | *My parents are …* |
| Mein(e) Vater/Mutter ist … | *My father/mother is …* |
| altmodisch | *old-fashioned* |
| lieb | *gentle, sweet, lovely* |
| modern | *modern* |
| streng | *strict* |
| tolerant | *tolerant* |
| ungeduldig | *impatient* |
| Wir verstehen uns (nicht) gut. | *We (don't) get on well.* |
| Das finde ich (nicht) … | *I (don't) think that's …* |
|   gut/schlecht/gemein. | *good/bad/mean.* |

## Was machst du zu Hause? — *How do you help at home?*

| | |
|---|---|
| Ich decke den Tisch. | *I set the table.* |
| Ich wasche ab. | *I do the washing-up.* |
| Ich putze das Badezimmer. | *I clean the bathroom.* |
| Ich füttere die Katze. | *I feed the cat.* |
| Ich sauge Staub. | *I do the vacuuming.* |
| Ich kaufe im Supermarkt ein. | *I go shopping in the supermarket.* |
| Ich räume mein Zimmer auf. | *I tidy my room.* |
| Wie oft machst du das? | *How often do you do that?* |
| jeden Tag | *every day* |
| einmal pro Woche | *once a week* |

## Warum bist du in Köln? — *Why are you in Cologne?*

| | |
|---|---|
| Was hast du gemacht? | *What did you do?* |
| Ich habe/Du hast/Er/Sie hat | *I/You/He/She …* |
|   Pizza/einen Test gemacht. | *made pizza/did a test.* |
|   ein Ticket/eine CD gekauft. | *bought a ticket/CD.* |
|   in der Disco getanzt. | *danced in the disco.* |
|   eine Anzeige/ein Buch gelesen. | *read an advert/book.* |
|   eine E-Mail/einen Brief geschrieben. | *wrote an email/a letter.* |
|   das Praktikum bekommen. | *got the work experience.* |
| Ich bin/Du bist/Er ist/Sie ist … | *I/You/He/She …* |
|   nach Zürich gefahren. | *went to Zurich.* |
|   in die Stadt/in den Park gegangen. | *went into town/to the park.* |

# Checklist

| How well do you think you can do the following? | | | |
|---|---|---|---|
| Write a sentence for each one if you can. | | | |
| | I can do this well | I can do this but not very well | I can't do this yet |
| 1. describe my own and other people's appearance and personality | | | |
| 2. say what I do to help at home | | | |
| 3. talk about what I've done recently | | | |
| 4. use the linking word *weil* | | | |
| 5. use the perfect tense | | | |
| 6. use different strategies to learn new words | | | |

**1** Write in the times. Find the missing time (in the tinted boxes down).

8:00

3:30

11:00

6:30

6:45

1:15

7:45

6:00

7:15

Missing time: _____

**2** Unjumble the sentences and write each one below the appropriate picture.

- stehe Ich auf
- nach fahre Hause Ich
- ins Ich Bett gehe
- frühstücke Ich
- wache auf Ich
- Zähne Ich meine putze

**a**

_____

**b**

_____

**c**

_____

**d**

_____

**e**

_____

**f**

_____

**1**  Write out these jumbled perfect tense sentences correctly.

**a**  Wir gefrühstückt haben acht um Uhr

Wir haben ..._____

**b**  Hannover Alex gefahren ist nach

_____

**c**  telefoniert Ich mit habe Mama

_____

**d**  Astrid gekocht Kaffee hat

_____

**e**  gegessen hast Du Bratwurst eine

_____

**f**  bin gegangen Ich Uhr zehn Bett um ins

_____

**2**  Now translate the sentences from Activity 1 into English.

**a**  _____  **d**  _____

**b**  _____  **e**  _____

**c**  _____  **f**  _____

**3**   Listen and decide in which order Almut did these things. Number them 1–7.

**a**   **b**   **c**   **d**

**e**   **f**   **g**

**4**   Listen again and answer these questions.

**a**  Why was she doing her homework in the morning?  _____

**b**  What trouble did she have on the bus?  _____

sauer = *annoyed*

**1**  Listen and write in figures the times being given by the radio announcer.

1 _____11.15_____  3 _____  5 _____  7 _____

2 _____  4 _____  6 _____  8 _____

**2** Write out these word snakes correctly. Some letters should be capitals, either because the words are nouns or because they begin the sentence. Alter them as necessary.

a ichhabemitmeinembrudertelefoniert.

Ich habe mit ...

_____

b wirhabenumhalbsiebenferngesehen.

_____

c ulihatumhalbzweiabgewaschen.

_____

d ichhabediekatzenichtgefüttert.

_____

e leohatheutemorgenradiozoomgehört.

_____

f hastdudeinee-mailsgecheckt?

_____

**3** Read these times out loud to your partner. Your partner should check that you have done them correctly. Then make up some more of your own.

a   b  c   d   e   f

# 1A.4 Es war super!

**1** 🎧 **Listen and answer the questions in English.**

**1** Where did Ahmed go? ___to a concert___

When? _____

What did he think of it? _____

**2** Who did Nina visit? _____

When? _____

What did she think of it? _____

**3** Where did Kathi do? _____

When? _____

What did she think of it? _____

**4** What did Max do? _____

When? _____

What did he think of it? _____

**2** **These opinion words are all written backwards. Sort them out, then translate each into English.**

| | | | | |
|---|---|---|---|---|
| **a** TTEN | ___nett___ | ___nice___ | ☐ |
| **b** MMILHCS | _____ | _____ | ☐ |
| **c** REPUS | _____ | _____ | ☐ |
| **d** TUG | _____ | _____ | ☐ |
| **e** TUAL | _____ | _____ | ☐ |
| **f** THCELHCS | _____ | _____ | ☐ |
| **g** TNASSERETNI | _____ | _____ | ☐ |
| **h** HCSIDOMTLA | _____ | _____ | ☐ |
| **i** GISSERTS | _____ | _____ | ☐ |
| **j** LOOC | _____ | _____ | ☐ |

**3** **When you have written out the words in Activity 2, put a cross by negative adjectives and a tick by positive ones.**

# 1A.5 Letztes Wochenende

**1** **Add an appropriate past participle to each sentence.**

a Wir haben Fußball _____ *gespielt* _____ .

b Bettina ist in die Disco _____ .

c Bist du im Schwimmbad _____ ?

d Ich bin oft nach Paris _____ .

e Papa hat eine neue Hose _____ .

f In Spanien haben wir Fotos _____ .

**2** **Now write six new perfect tense sentences like those in Activity 1, but using new vocabulary of your choice.**

_____

_____

_____

_____

_____

_____

**3** **Answer these questions for yourself. (The answers don't have to be true!)**

a Was hast du am Wochenende gemacht?

_____

b Was hast du am Samstag gemacht?

_____

c Was hast du am Sonntag gemacht?

_____

> Try to say things you really did. For new vocabulary you need, use a dictionary (there are some great online dictionaries) or ask your teacher.

**Separable and reflexive verbs**

The infinitive of some German verbs needs to be split into two parts when used in the present tense. These are called **separable** verbs – *trennbare Verben*: **abwaschen** – Ich **wasche ab**. (*I wash up.*)

In the perfect tense, the prefix stays at the front of the verb, before **ge-**: Ich habe **abgewaschen**. (*I washed up.*)

With other German verbs, called **reflexive** verbs or *reflexive Verben*, you need to use an extra pronoun. The pronoun that goes with *ich* is *mich* (myself): sich setzen – Ich setze **mich** auf den Stuhl. (*I sit down on the chair.*)

A few verbs are both separable and reflexive: sich anziehen – Ich ziehe **mich an**. (*I get dressed.*)

**1** **Which of these sentences contains a <u>reflexive</u> verb?**
**Put a tick by those which do.**
**Put a cross by any verb which is <u>separable</u>.**

| | | | | |
|---|---|---|---|---|
| **a** Ich ziehe mich an. | ✓ ☐ | **f** Ich ziehe mich aus. | ☐ ☐ |
| **b** Ich wasche ab. | ☐ ☐ | **g** Ich sehe fern. | ☐ ☐ |
| **c** Ich gehe ins Bett. | ☐ ☐ | **h** Ich räume auf. | ☐ ☐ |
| **d** Ich frühstücke. | ☐ ☐ | **i** Ich stehe auf. | ☐ ☐ |
| **e** Ich wasche mich. | ☐ ☐ | **j** Ich kaufe ein. | |

**2** **Translate the sentences in Activity 1 into English.**

**a** _____    **f** _____

**b** _____    **g** _____

**c** _____    **h** _____

**d** _____    **i** _____

**e** _____    **j** _____

**3** **Put the right past participles (including prefix) into these sentences.**

**a** Ich habe _____ . (*watched TV*)

**b** Ich habe _____ . (*washed up*)

**c** Ich habe _____ . (*cleared up*)

## Understanding times

**1** 🎧 **Listen and note the times when Erwin does the things illustrated.**

a  7.00

b

c

d

e

f

**2** **Say these times in German to your partner and get him or her to write them down in figures instantly, without time for thought.**

> half past ten    half past five    half past three    half past nine

The German way of saying 'half past' can be tricky for learners. It can make you arrive an hour late, if you're not careful!

## Reading for detail

**3** **Read about Simone's weekend, then correct the wrong sentences below. Give details where you can.**

> Hallo! Ich heiße Simone. Letztes Wochenende war toll!
> Ich bin am Samstag mit meiner Schwester mit dem Zug nach München gefahren. Zu Mittag haben wir in einem neuen China-Restaurant gegessen, das war echt lecker. Am Nachmittag haben wir bei H&M Kleider gekauft. Ich habe ein rotes T-Shirt gekauft und Monika hat eine schöne Jacke gefunden, die war ganz billig. Wir sind um 18 Uhr nach Hause gefahren.
> Am Sonntag waren wir sportlich. Wir haben im Garten Tennis gespielt – drei Stunden lang! Wir waren ganz schön kaputt, das kann ich dir sagen!!

**a** Simone went to Munich on her own. _She went with her sister._

**b** She didn't enjoy her lunch. _____

**c** She went shopping in the morning. _____

**d** The shopping trip was unsuccessful. _____

**e** She went home on foot. _____

**f** On Sunday she lazed around. _____

| Mein Alltag | My daily routine |
|---|---|
| Ich wache auf. | I wake up. |
| Ich stehe auf. | I get up. |
| Ich wasche mich. | I have a wash. |
| Ich putze meine Zähne. | I brush my teeth. |
| Ich ziehe mich an. | I get dressed. |
| Ich frühstücke. | I have breakfast. |
| Ich fahre zur Arbeit. | I go to work. |
| Ich fahre nach Hause. | I go home. |
| Ich ziehe mich aus. | I get undressed. |
| Ich gehe ins Bett. | I go to bed. |

| Wie spät ist es? | What time is it? |
|---|---|
| Es ist Viertel vor acht. | It's quarter to eight. |
| Es ist acht Uhr. | It's eight o'clock. |
| Es ist Viertel nach acht. | It's quarter past eight. |
| Es ist halb neun. | It's half past eight. |

| Was hast du gemacht? | What did you do? |
|---|---|
| Was hast du gestern gemacht? | What did you do yesterday? |
| Ich habe … | I … |
| CDs gekauft. | bought CDs. |
| E-Mails gelesen. | read emails. |
| Fußball gespielt. | played football. |
| Hausaufgaben gemacht. | did homework. |
| Kaffee gekocht. | made coffee. |
| Musik gehört. | listened to music. |
| eine Nachricht geschrieben. | wrote a message. |
| Pizza gegessen. | ate pizza. |
| getanzt. | danced. |
| telefoniert. | talked on the phone. |
| Ich bin … | I … |
| ins Kino gegangen. | went to the cinema. |
| in die Stadt gefahren. | went into town. |

| Und gestern Abend …? | And yesterday evening …? |
|---|---|
| Es ist …/Um … | It is …/At … |
| neunzehn Uhr fünfunddreißig | 19.35 |
| siebzehn Uhr zwanzig | 17.20 |
| achtzehn Uhr zehn | 18.10 |
| zwanzig Uhr fünf | 20.05 |
| dreizehn Uhr fünfundfünfzig | 13.55 |

| Ich habe … | I … |
|---|---|
| aufgeräumt. | tidied up. |
| abgewaschen. | did the washing-up. |
| ferngesehen. | watched TV. |

| Es war super! | It was great! |
|---|---|
| Es/Das Konzert war … | It/The concert was … |
| Die Arbeit/Die Woche war … | Work/The week was … |
| anstrengend | tiring, exhausting |
| gut | good |
| interessant | interesting |

| | |
|---|---|
| langweilig | boring |
| laut | loud, noisy |
| nett | nice |
| schlecht | bad |
| schlimm | awful |
| schwer | difficult, hard |
| stressig | stressful |
| super | super, great |
| toll | great |

| Letztes Wochenende | Last weekend |
|---|---|
| Ich habe … | I … |
| Fotos geschickt. | sent photos. |
| Freunde getroffen/besucht. | met/visited friends. |
| ein Konzert besucht. | went to a concert. |
| gearbeitet. | worked. |
| gechattet. | chatted. |
| gegessen/getrunken. | ate/drank … |
| gewohnt. | stayed/lived … |
| mich entspannt. | relaxed. |
| Ich bin geschwommen. | I swam. |

## Checklist

| How well do you think you can do the following? | | | |
|---|---|---|---|
| Write a sentence for each one if you can. | | | |
| | I can do this well | I can do this but not very well | I can't do this yet |
| 1. describe my daily routine | | | |
| 2. tell the time | | | |
| 3. describe what I've done recently and give my opinion | | | |
| 4. use reflexive and separable verbs | | | |
| 5. use the perfect tense with *haben* and *sein* | | | |
| 6. use the imperfect tense (*Es war …*) | | | |

**1** Solve the clues and write the words in the grid. What is the missing festival (in the tinted box down)?

1 Flames (on a German river)

2 Unity Day (part 1)

3 A new year begins

4 Unity Day (part 2)

5 A festive date in December

6 Unity Day (part 3)

7 Good for bunnies!

8 Presents today in Germany

Missing festival: _____

**2** Find in the box below the best endings to these sentences.

a Ich finde Heiligabend super, _____ weil man viele... _____

b Ich mag Ostern, _____

c Partys mag ich nicht, _____

d Fasching macht Spaß, _____

e Silvester ist toll, _____

f Ich finde Weihnachten gut, _____

> weil ich schüchtern bin.
> weil ein neuer Jahr beginnt.
> weil es viel gutes Essen gibt.
>
> weil man sich verkleidet.
> weil ich gern Schokolade esse.
> weil man viele Geschenke bekommt.

# 1B.2 Party machen

**1** **Fill the gaps in these sentences. The English words in brackets tell you which verbs to use.**

**a** Ich _____kann_____ gut Tennis _____spielen_____ . (*can play*)

**b** Wir _____ um 22 Uhr ins Bett _____ . (*must go*)

**c** Wir _____ Hausaufgaben _____ . (*must do*)

**d** Paul _____ gut _____ . (*can sing*)

**e** Bettina _____ eine Party _____ . (*must organise*)

**f** Ich _____ nicht _____ . (*can't come*)

**g** Wir _____ Spaß _____ . (*can have*)

**h** Berni _____ _____ . (*must wash up*)

**2**  **Listen and note down either <u>can</u> or <u>must</u>, plus the activity (in English).**

1 _____can_____ _____go to town_____

2 _____ _____

3 _____ _____

4 _____ _____

5 _____ _____

6 _____ _____

7 _____ _____

8 _____ _____

**3** **Now write three sentences of your own, similar to those you have just heard, using *können* or *müssen*.**

_____

_____

_____

# 1B.3 Nichts als Ausreden

**1**   **Underline all the <u>modal verbs</u> in the text.**
**Write them out, in English, in the order in which they appear.**

> Leo: Letztes Jahr hat Sira eine Faschingsparty organisiert. Das war toll. Dieses Jahr will Sira die Party nicht organisieren, also muss ich es machen. Das finde ich aber schwer! Ich soll alles einkaufen. Das ist ein Problem für mich, weil ich kein Geld habe. Wir wollen Karaoke singen, aber ich kann nicht gut singen. Ich will im Wohnzimmer feiern, aber meine Tante sagt, das darf ich nicht. Sie sagt auch, wir dürfen nicht trinken, nicht rauchen und nicht laut sein. Das wollen wir natürlich nicht! Und am nächsten Morgen muss ich alles aufräumen. Weißt du was? Ich organisiere keine Party!

Modal verbs, in English: _____

**2**   **Read Leo's text again and answer the questions. Give details where possible.**

**a**  Why isn't Sira organising the party? _She doesn't want to._

**b**  What's Leo's problem with shopping? _____

**c**  And what's his problem with karaoke? _____

**d**  Why can't they have the party in the living room? _____

**e**  What aren't they allowed to do at the party? _____

**f**  What does Leo say about that? _____

**g**  What would he have to do the next day? _____

**h**  What conclusion does he reach?_____

**3**   **Write two replies to invitations.**

**a**  I'd like to come, thanks for the invitation.

_____

**b**  Unfortunately I can't come.

_____

# 1B.4 Die Party war spitze!

**1** 🎧 **Listen to a description of a disastrous party. Answer the questions.**

**a** How many people came to the party? _four_

**b** Why was that? _____

**c** What did they do at the party? _____

**d** Was it fun? _____

**e** What was the music like? _____

**f** And the food? _____

**g** How did Olli disgrace himself? Give details. _____

_____

**2** **Here's a description of a better party. Fill in the gaps with suitable words from the box.**

**a** Die Party _war_ spitze.

**b** Wir haben Einladungen _____ .

**c** Sandra hat Kuchen _____ .

**d** Hakan hat Musik _____ .

**e** Wir haben 50 Gäste _____ .

**f** Es _____ viel zu essen und zu trinken.

**g** Wir _____ alle viel Spaß.

**h** Ich _____ eine tolle Party machen und die Party _____ auch toll!

> wollte  hatten  eingeladen  geschrieben
> war  gebacken  gab  gespielt

**3** **Which of the words you used in Activity 2 are past participles?**

_____

**1** *Dezemberquiz.* **Find ten December festival words in this grid.**

| K | U | C | H | E | N | C | Ü | A | E | N | H |
|---|---|---|---|---|---|---|---|---|---|---|---|
| R | G | S | S | T | I | E | F | E | L | K | E |
| N | E | I | ß | I | K | E | R | O | E | N | I |
| A | M | L | G | M | O | Z | Ö | B | ß | U | L |
| Z | D | V | A | U | L | C | I | A | D | G | I |
| F | E | E | T | H | A | W | J | U | Ö | L | G |
| O | Z | S | E | Z | U | F | T | M | V | F | A |
| A | E | T | G | E | S | C | H | E | N | K | B |
| L | M | E | A | K | W | C | W | G | I | O | E |
| I | B | R | Ö | E | B | ß | G | K | A | Ü | N |
| W | E | I | H | N | A | C | H | T | E | N | D |
| L | R | T | C | F | H | E | N | A | D | K | S |

The words you are looking for are the German equivalents of:

| Christmas | present | December | St Nicolas (Dec 6) | goose |
|---|---|---|---|---|
| New Year's Eve | tree | cake | Christmas Eve | boot |

**2** **Fill the gaps with the right question words.**

**a** _____ Geschenke hast du bekommen? – Zehn!

**b** _____ essen wir heute? – Gans.

**c** _____ ist der Kuchen? – Auf dem Tisch.

**d** _____ hat das Essen gekocht? – Mein Vater.

**e** _____ öffnen wir die Geschenke? – Um 18 Uhr.

**f** _____ kommen wir nach Hause? – Mit dem Auto.

## Modal verbs

Modal verbs (*können, müssen, dürfen, wollen, sollen*) are used for saying what you **can**, **must**, **are allowed to**, **want to** or **should** do.

A modal verb is always the second idea in a German sentence. It is usually followed by an infinitive at the end of the sentence. For more details, see page 46 of your Student Book.

**1** Fill in the gaps with modal verbs as indicated by the English words in brackets.

a Ich _____will_____ zur Party gehen, aber ich _____ es nicht. (*want, am allowed*)

b Wir _____ nicht abwaschen, aber wir _____ es tun. (*want, must*)

c Olli _____ gut in Mathe sein, aber er _____ es nicht. (*want, can*)

d _____ du gut Skateboard fahren? – Nein, aber ich _____ es lernen. (*can, want*)

e Ich _____ Hausaufgaben machen, aber ich _____ sie nicht machen! (*should, want*)

f _____ du ins Kino gehen? – Nein, das _____ ich nicht. Ich _____ zu Hause bleiben. (*want, am allowed, must*)

## The imperfect tense

The imperfect tense, for example *war* (was), *hatte* (had), is used for descriptions in the past.

**sein:** ich war, du warst, er/sie/es war, wir waren, ihr wart, sie/Sie waren

**haben:** ich hatte, du hattest, er/sie/es hatte, wir hatten, ihr hattet, sie/Sie hatten

**2** Translate these sentences into German, using the imperfect tense of *haben* and *sein*.

a I had a computer. _____Ich hatte..._____

b We were at home. _____

c Hugo had new shoes. _____

d Sigrid wasn't very healthy. _____

e He had a Christmas cake. _____

f We had lots of presents. _____

g I was at school. _____

h Were you ill? _____

## Grammar patterns

**1** This unit has practised some key grammar patterns.
Pattern 1. Ich finde Fasching cool, weil es Spaß macht.
**Join each pair of sentences with *weil*:**

**a** Ich mag Weihnachten. Man bekommt Geschenke.

_____

**b** Ich finde Ostern toll. Ich mag Schokolade.

_____

**c** Nina mag Partys nicht. Sie sind zu laut.

_____

**d** Ich war nicht zu Hause. Ich war in Berlin.

_____

**e** Linda war krank. Sie hat einen schlechten Hamburger gegessen.

_____

**f** Wir müssen nach Hause gehen. Es ist spät.

_____

**2** Pattern 2. Ich muss eine neue Hose kaufen.
**Which four other modal verbs have you learnt, apart from *müssen*?**

_____  _____  _____  _____

**3** Complete these sentences:

**a** Ich backe Kuchen. Ich kann ___Kuchen___ ___backen___ .

**b** Wir gehen zur Party. Wir dürfen _____ _____ _____ .

**c** Ali macht Hausaufgaben. Ali muss _____ _____ .

**d** Ich gehe ins Kino. Ich will _____ _____ _____ .

**e** Du parkst hier nicht. Du sollst _____ _____ _____ .

**4** Now write three sentences about things you *must*, *should* and *can* do.

_____

_____

| Feiertage und Feste | *National holidays and festivals* |
| --- | --- |
| Fasching | *Carnival* |
| Heiligabend | *Christmas Eve* |
| Neujahr | *New Year* |
| Ostern | *Easter* |
| Rhein in Flammen | *Rhine in Flames* |
| Silvester | *New Year's Eve* |
| Tag der Deutschen Einheit | *Day of German Unity* |
| Weihnachten | *Christmas* |
| | |
| Wann feiert man …? | *When do you celebrate …?* |
| Man feiert am (+ *date*) … | *We celebrate … on the (+ date).* |
| | |
| Wie findest du …? | *What do you think of …?* |
| Ich finde … klasse. | *I think … is great.* |
| stark | *great, really cool, wicked* |
| supergut | *fantastic, excellent* |

**Party machen** — *Organising a party*

| Ich muss … | *I must …* |
| --- | --- |
| Einladungen schreiben. | *write invitations.* |
| Kuchen backen. | *bake cakes.* |
| Musik auswählen. | *choose some music.* |
| ein Outfit kaufen. | *buy an outfit.* |
| das Zimmer dekorieren. | *decorate the room.* |
| Essen kaufen. | *buy food.* |
| aufräumen. | *tidy up.* |
| Man kann … kaufen. | *You can buy …* |
| in der Bäckerei | *at the baker's* |
| im Modegeschäft | *at the clothes shop* |
| | |
| Man kann … | *You can …* |
| Karaoke singen. | *sing karaoke.* |
| Spaß haben. | *have fun.* |
| mit Freunden reden. | *chat with friends.* |
| tanzen. | *dance.* |
| essen/trinken. | *eat/drink.* |

**Nichts als Ausreden** — *Excuses, excuses …*

| Ich mache eine Strandparty. | *I'm having a beach party.* |
| --- | --- |
| Kommst du? | *Will you come?* |
| Ja, gern. Vielen Dank für die Einladung. | *Yes, I'd love to. Thanks very much for the invitation.* |
| Nein, ich darf leider nicht kommen. | *No, unfortunately I'm not allowed to come.* |
| Ich soll … | *I'm supposed to …* |
| Hausaufgaben machen. | *do my homework.* |
| mein Zimmer aufräumen. | *tidy my room.* |
| zu Hause helfen. | *help at home.* |
| im Garten arbeiten. | *work in the garden.* |
| auf meine Geschwister aufpassen. | *look after my brothers and sisters.* |

**Die Party war spitze!** — *The party was great!*

| langweilig | *boring* |
| --- | --- |
| spitze/toll | *great* |
| der totale Hammer | *totally cool, awesome* |
| | |
| Ich hatte hundert Gäste. | *I had a hundred guests.* |
| Es gab … | *There was/were …* |
| eine Karaoke-Anlage. | *a karaoke machine.* |
| leckeres Essen. | *delicious food.* |
| nette Gäste. | *nice guests.* |
| tolle Musik. | *great music.* |
| | |
| Ich habe … | *I …* |
| Einladungen geschrieben. | *wrote invitations.* |
| Musik ausgewählt. | *chose some music.* |
| das Studio dekoriert. | *decorated the studio.* |
| Essengekauft. | *bought food.* |
| gebacken. | *baked.* |
| | |
| Wir/Die Gäste haben … | *We/The guests …* |
| Musik gehört. | *listened to music.* |
| gesungen/getanzt. | *sang/danced.* |
| gefeiert/gegessen/ getrunken. | *celebrated/ate/drank …* |

# Checklist

| How well do you think you can do the following? | | | |
| --- | --- | --- | --- |
| Write a sentence for each one if you can. | | | |
| | I can do this well | I can do this but not very well | I can't do this yet |
| 1. talk about national holidays / festivals | | | |
| 2. talk about organising a party and describe a party I've been to | | | |
| 3. accept or decline an invitation, and give excuses | | | |
| 4. use modal verbs | | | |
| 5. use the imperfect tense and the perfect tense | | | |
| 6. use different strategies to help with listening | | | |

**1** Work out what type of programme each one is and write it in.

## TV Heute – Samstag, 25. Juni

15.00 Blitz-Info

Nachrichten

19.00 Meyerstraße

_____

22.00 Rocktastisch

_____

15.30 Fragen, Fragen

_____

19.30 Maxi Maus

_____

23.00 Handball

_____

16.30 Bist du ein Star?

_____

20.00 Infos um acht

_____

18.00 Tiger in Indien

_____

20.30 Kleine Schwester

_____

Realityshow
Musiksendung
Nachrichten
Quizsendung
Sportsendung
Seifenoper
Castingshow
Dokumentarserie
Zeichentrickserie

**2** Work with a partner. Say what kind of TV show you want to watch. Your partner should guide you to the appropriate show.

Example: **A** Ich will eine Seifenoper sehen.

**B** Es gibt „Meyerstraße" um 19 Uhr.

**1** Unjumble these anagrams of technology-related words. When you have worked them out, write them in the grid. What's the missing word in the tinted box down?

1 AKOECOFB  _Facebook_

2 NYAHD  _____

3 ATPLPO  _____

4 TDPOANE  _____

5 ENNITRET  _____

6 NENOLI  _____

7 PIOD  _____

8 MTPUEOCR  _____

Missing word:  _____

**2** Look again at the words in the grid above and answer these questions.

a  What do you notice about the words (in view of the fact that you are learning German)?

_____

b  Which do you think is the odd one out, and why?

_____

c  By contrast, what do you notice about these words relating to 'old media': *Fernsehen, Zeitung, Schreibmaschine, Brief*?

_____

d  *Fernsehen* and *Schreibmaschine* are examples of words being put together to form new ones. Explain the components of these two words and how they come to make new ones.

_____

e  In what way is the word *Brief* a false friend?

_____

# 2A.3  Techno ist toll!

**1**  *Musikquiz.*  Find 12 music-related words in this wordsearch.

| D | U | B | S | T | E | P | H | A |
|---|---|---|---|---|---|---|---|---|
| I | Ö | L | I | ß | L | O | F | O |
| S | A | U | G | G | E | P | A | K |
| C | B | E | N | H | C | T | C | Z |
| O | M | S | W | J | T | O | L | K |
| R | B | Ü | U | B | R | K | E | L |
| F | O | L | K | H | O | U | S | E |
| U | T | E | C | H | N | O | F | T |
| N | P | I | N | D | I | E | K | L |
| K | C | D | I | ß | C | J | D | U |
| S | R | E | G | G | A | E | S | Ü |

### Heiko Heimlich spielt Fußball in der Bundesliga, aber er mag auch gern Musik.

Heiko, welche Musik hörst du am liebsten?

Also, ich höre besonders gern Techno. Hier in Berlin gibt es viele Techno-Clubs, wo man die ganze Nacht tanzen kann. Das ist natürlich nicht gut für mein Trainingsprogramm und normalerweise gehe ich um elf Uhr nach Hause!

Kannst du singen?

Ja, ganz gut. Ich singe manchmal Karaoke mit den anderen Spielern in meinem Verein. Ich kann auch E-Gitarre spielen, aber nicht sehr gut. Mein Bruder Hans Heimlich ist in einer Band.

Welche Musik gefällt dir nicht?

Klassische Musik höre ich nicht gern, weil diese Musik zu langsam und zu leise ist. Techno und Metal finde ich besser, weil sie laut und schnell sind, wie Fußball!

**2**  Read the article below and answer these questions in English.

  **a**  What kind of music does Heiko like and why is that convenient?

  _____

  **b**  What does he say about training? Give details.

  _____

  **c**  What does he say about singing? Give details.

  _____

  **d**  What music doesn't he like? Give details.

  _____

  **e**  What's he saying in the last sentence?

  _____

**1** 🎧 Listen to Anne and Leo discussing films and fill in the grid. Find out the type of film, the country it comes from, the cinema showing it, and what they say about it.

| Film | Type | Country | Cinema | Described as |
|------|------|---------|--------|--------------|
| *Der Blaue Planet* | | | | |
| *Mein Schatz* | | | | |
| *Lachen in Lyon* | | | | |

**2** 🎧 Listen again to spot these expressions. What do they mean in English?

*Gute Idee.* _____

*So was finde ich doof.* _____

*Ich gehe online.* _____

**3** Imagine you've seen the three films above. Write what you thought of each one. Add as many details and opinions as you want. Use this pattern:

Ich habe _____ (*film title*) gesehen. Das war ein(e) _____ (*film type*).
Der Film hat mir (nicht) gefallen, weil er _____ (*description*) war.

_____

_____

_____

_____

_____

_____

_____

**1** **Look at these reading materials. How would you describe each one in German?**

Lotti Lamm ist
ein Kinderbuch.

_____

_____

_____

_____

_____

Sachbuch

Mädchenzeitschrift

Liebesroman

Kinderbuch

Krimi

Sportmagazin

**2** 🎧 **Listen to the results of a radio survey about young people's reading habits. Note the results in the grid, in the order you hear them.**

| Percentage % | Type of reading material (in English) |
|---|---|
| 15 | |
| | |
| | |
| | |
| | |
| | |

What's the least popular reading material and why?

_____

**Possessive adjectives**

|  | masculine | feminine | neuter | plural |
|---|---|---|---|---|
| *my* | mein | meine | mein | meine |
| *your* | dein | deine | dein | deine |
| *his* | sein | seine | sein | seine |
| *her* | ihr | ihre | ihr | ihre |

**1** **Write in the correct form of the possessive adjective given in brackets.**

**a** _____Seine_____ Brille ist kaputt. (*his*)

**b** War _____ Essen okay? (*your*)

**c** _____ Lieblingssänger ist Bruno Mars. (*his*)

**d** _____ Lieblingssendung ist X Factor. (*my*)

**e** _____ Lieblingsfilm ist Toy Story. (*her*)

**f** Ist das _____ Handy? (*your*)

**g** _____ Freunde sind alle nett. (*my*)

**h** Sie heißt Manja und das ist _____ Freundin. (*her*)

| masculine | feminine | neuter | plural |
|---|---|---|---|
| Sänger | Brille | Essen | Freunde |
| Film | Sendung | Handy | |
| | Freundin | | |

**Demonstrative adjectives**

The words *dieser/diese/dieses/diese* can be used in place of *der/die/das/die* if you want to say 'this' or 'that', 'these' or 'those':

**masculine:** dieser      **neuter:** dieses

**feminine:** diese      **plural:** diese

**2** **Use *dieser, dieses* or *diese* in these sentences:**

**a** _____Dieses_____ Eis schmeckt toll.

**b** _____ Sänger kann nicht gut singen.

**c** _____ Buch ist interessant.

**d** _____ Laptops sind viel zu teuer.

**e** _____ Webseite ist neu.

**f** _____ Musik ist sehr laut.

**g** _____ Film ist altmodisch.

**h** _____ Boygroups sind furchtbar.

| masculine | feminine | neuter | plural |
|---|---|---|---|
| Sänger | Webseite | Eis | Laptops |
| Film | Musik | Buch | Boygroups |

# 2A.6ʙ Think

**Die Sprache der Technologie**
The language of technology is international. Because many of the products originated in America, English words are often used in other languages such as German. What often changes, however, is the pronunciation.

**1** **Say these words out loud in the way they would be pronounced by a German speaker.**

🎧 **Check by listening to the recording.**

| | |
|---|---|
| Webseite | Medien |
| Internet | Blog |
| Videoclip | Laptop |
| Facebook | chatten |
| MP3-Player | Kanal |
| Handy | |

**2** **Sort the technology words in Activity 1 into the three categories in the table below.**

| Exactly the same as in English | Similar to English words | Completely different |
|---|---|---|
| | | |

**3** **Complete the sentences using a second adjective or adverb which means the <u>opposite</u> of the first one. (Check Unit 2A *Vokabular* if you need ideas.)**

a Der Sessel ist bequem, aber der Stuhl ist _____ unbequem _____ .

b Schokolade schmeckt gut, aber Lakritze schmeckt _____ .

c Papier ist billig, aber Gold ist _____ .

d Geschichte ist interessant, aber Mathe ist _____ .

e Dieter ist doof, aber Daniel ist _____ .

f Latein ist kompliziert, aber Englisch ist _____ .

g Ein Hase läuft schnell, aber eine Schildkröte geht _____ .

• You may not agree with all the opinions in those sentences. Write some sentences of your own, using pairs of adjectives and saying what you really think.

_____

_____

_____

_____

## Im Fernsehen — On TV

| | |
|---|---|
| eine Castingshow | a talent show |
| eine Dokumentarserie | a documentary |
| eine Musiksendung | a music programme |
| die Nachrichten | the news |
| eine Quizsendung | a quiz show |
| eine Realityshow | a reality show |
| eine Seifenoper | a soap opera |
| eine Sportsendung | a sports programme |
| eine Zeichentrickserie | a cartoon |
| Ich sehe (nicht) gern … | I (don't) like watching … |
| Meine Lieblingssendung ist … | My favourite programme is … |

## Neue Medien, alte Medien — New media, old media

| | |
|---|---|
| das Chatten auf Skype | chatting on Skype |
| der Fernseher | television set |
| das Handy, das Telefon | mobile phone, telephone |
| die Schreibmaschine | typewriter |
| die Tageszeitung | daily paper |

| | |
|---|---|
| Ich höre Radio auf meinem Player/iPod. | I listen to the radio on my MP3 player/iPod. |
| Ich sehe Filme auf meinem Computer. | I watch films on my computer. |
| Ich lese im Internet. | I read on the internet. |
| Ich lade Videoclips aus dem Internet herunter. | I download video clips from the internet. |
| Ich chatte mit Freunden im Internet. | I chat with friends on the Internet. |

| | |
|---|---|
| weil das schnell/langsam geht | because it's fast/slow |
| bequem | convenient |
| billig, teuer | cheap, expensive |
| einfach, kompliziert | easy, complicated |
| langweilig | boring |
| praktisch, unpraktisch | practical, impractical |
| Das kostet nichts/viel. | It costs nothing/a lot. |

| | |
|---|---|
| morgens, mittags | in the mornings, at midday |
| nachmittags, abends | in the afternoons/evenings |
| jeden Tag/Abend, jede Woche | every day/evening/week |
| oft, manchmal, selten, nie | often, sometimes, seldom, never |

## Techno ist toll! — Techno is great!

| | |
|---|---|
| Welcher/Welche/Welches … gefällt dir (am besten)? | Which … do you like (best)? |
| … gefällt mir gut/gar nicht. | I like … /don't like … at all. |
| Ich höre am liebsten … | I prefer listening to … |
| die Band, die Gruppe | band, group |
| das Lied | song |
| der Sänger/die Sängerin | singer (male/female) |
| der Schlagzeuger | drummer |

## Wie war der Film? — What was the film like?

| | |
|---|---|
| Welchen Film hast du gesehen? | What film have you seen? |
| Ich habe … gesehen. | I saw … |
| Was für ein Film ist/war das? | What kind of film is/was it? |
| ein Actionfilm | an action film |
| ein Dokumentarfilm | a documentary |
| ein Fantasyfilm | a fantasy film |
| eine Komödie | a comedy |
| ein Liebesfilm | a love story |
| ein Musical | a musical |
| ein Science-Fiction-Film | a science fiction film |
| ein Zeichentrickfilm | a cartoon |

| | |
|---|---|
| Dieser Film gefällt mir | I like this film, … |
| Dieser Film hat mir (nicht) gefallen, … | I liked/didn't like this film … |
| weil er lustig ist/war. | because it is/was funny. |
| weil die Spezialeffekte toll sind/waren. | because the special effects are/ were great. |

| | |
|---|---|
| die Geschichte | story/plot |
| der Schauspieler/die Schauspielerin | actor/actress |
| romantisch | romantic |
| spannend | exciting |
| unterhaltsam | entertaining |

# Checklist

| How well do you think you can do the following? | | | |
|---|---|---|---|
| Write a sentence for each one if you can. | | | |
| | I can do this well | I can do this but not very well | I can't do this yet |
| 1. talk about TV programmes, films, music and bands | | | |
| 2. talk about old and new forms of media | | | |
| 3. talk about my reading habits | | | |
| 4. use the perfect tense and the imperfect | | | |
| 5. use strategies to help me understand longer texts | | | |
| 6. pronounce the *ei* and *ie* sounds | | | |

# 2B.1 Mein Lieblingshobby

**1** **Write in the correct form of *spielen* or *fahren* (present tense).**

**a** Ich _____spiele_____ oft Fußball mit meinen Freunden.

**b** Mein Freund _____ Schlagzeug in einer Rockgruppe.

**c** _____ du Gitarre? – Ja, ich _____ sehr gut.

**d** Ich _____ gern in den Alpen Ski.

**e** Ich _____ auch gern Rad, wenn ich Zeit habe.

**f** Wir _____ im Sommer Tennis.

**g** Olaf _____ oft am Wochenende Skateboard.

**h** Er _____ auch in seinem Zimmer Computerspiele.

**2** **Identify the German leisure activity words from the English clues.**

**a** Skiing on water _____

**b** Rolling on shoes _____

**c** A kind of VW _____

**d** Bike for racing _____

**e** Tennis on a table _____

**f** A jazz instrument _____

**3** 🎧 **Listen to Ben and Simone talking about their hobbies.
Note the details in the grid, in English.**

|  | **Ben** | **Simone** |
|---|---|---|
| likes | Ice-skating |  |
| reason |  |  |
| doesn't like |  |  |
| reason |  |  |

**Christian:** Mein Lieblingshobby ist Sport. Am Wochenende habe ich Tischtennis gespielt, aber ich habe leider nicht gewonnen. Wenn ich Zeit habe, spiele ich Golf mit meinem Vater oder manchmal gehe ich schwimmen, denn das Hallenbad ist nicht sehr weit von meinem Haus. Ich mag Tennis und ich fahre auch gern Rollschuh, weil das Spaß macht. Also bin ich ganz schön fit!

**1** Read the text above and underline all the connectives.

**2** Now write the German connectives next to their English meanings.

   **a** whenever / if _____

   **b** because (2 words) _____ _____

   **c** but _____

   **d** and _____

   **e** or _____

   **f** therefore _____

**3** Answer these questions about the text above in German.

   **a** Was hat Christian am Wochenende gemacht?

     _Er hat ..._ _____

   **b** Hat er gewonnen?

     _____

   **c** Schwimmt er im Freibad*?

     _____

   **d** Was macht er, wenn er Zeit hat?

     _____

   **e** Warum fährt er gern Rollschuh?

     _____

\* Freibad = *open-air pool*

**1** *Wetterquiz.* **Find the German for these ten weather words in the grid:**

| | | | | |
|---|---|---|---|---|
| storm | hot | snow | warm | sunny |
| rain | fog | wind | cold | summer |

| A | K | O | N | N | M | G | H |
|---|---|---|---|---|---|---|---|
| T | S | S | C | H | N | E | E |
| H | S | O | M | M | E | W | I |
| Z | Ü | N | D | R | B | I | ß |
| W | I | N | D | J | E | T | S |
| A | L | I | K | A | L | T | C |
| R | E | G | E | N | Ü | E | H |
| M | S | O | M | M | E | R | B |

**2** **Fill the gaps in these sentences.**

**a** Wenn es _____ ist, _____ ich Schlittschuh.

**b** Wenn es _____ ist, _____ ich in den Park.

**c** Wenn es _____ , _____ ich zu Hause.

**d** Wenn es _____ ist, _____ ich mit dem Bus,

nicht mit dem Auto.

**3** 🎧 **Listen and fill in the grid in English.**

| Season | Weather | Destination | Activity |
|---|---|---|---|
| winter | | | |
| | | | |
| | | | |

**1** 🎧 **Listen and note the past, present and future activities in the grid, in English.**

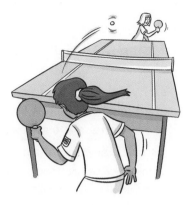

|   | Present | Past | Future |
|---|---------|------|--------|
| 1 | football |  |  |
| 2 |  |  |  |
| 3 |  |  |  |

**2** **Unjumble these future tense sentences.**

**a** wird mit Leo fahren Bus dem morgen

Leo wird ...

**b** gehen Wochenende Sira Kino ins am wird

**c** werde Freunden Ich spielen mit Federball meinen

**d** Spaghetti Abend werde kochen heute Ich

**e** Stadthalle werden hören der Rockmusik Wir in

**f** Skateboard morgen Park fahren werden Wir im

**3** **Translate these future tense sentences into German.**

**a** I'll play drums. _Ich werde ..._

**b** I'll play basketball.

**c** I'll read a magazine.

**d** I'll go to school.

**e** I'll drive to Bremen.

## „ISCHA FREIMAAK!"

In Süddeutschland gibt es Karneval, aber in der norddeutschen Hafenstadt Bremen feiert man immer im Oktober Freimarkt.

Der große Rummelplatz ist hinter der Stadthalle und nicht weit vom Bürgerpark. Tausende von Menschen besuchen den Freimarkt. Es gibt Riesenkarussells und eine große Achterbahn.

Es gibt viel zu essen und zu trinken. Für die Kinder gibt es Pferdewürste, Zuckerwatte, Sahneeis, Pommes mit Mayo, Kartoffelpuffer mit Apfelmus, und für die Eltern gibt es Glühwein und viel Bier im Bayernzelt.

Wie beim Fasching gibt es einen großen Umzug durch die Innenstadt. Die Leute werfen Bonbons auf die Straße und die Kinder sind sehr glücklich!

**1**  Read through the text above. It may seem a bit hard, but it's fun to work out meanings and it's easier than it seems, especially as the German language tends to put words together to make new ones. Try these activities to help you work out the unfamiliar words.

**a**  Bremen is quite near the sea. What do you think a *Hafenstadt* is?

_____

**b**  We're talking about a festival, like *Karneval*. What could a *Rummelplatz* be?

_____

**c**  Is the *Bürgerpark* somewhere to eat fast food? Look up *Bürger* in the

dictionary and work it out. _____

**d**  What's a *Karussell*? It's like an English word. _____

**e**  Guess what *Achterbahn* could mean. Remember *Bahn* means railway.

_____

**f**  What's a *Pferdewurst*? _____

**g**  If *Zucker* means 'sugar' and *Watte* means 'cotton wool', what is *Zuckerwatte*?

_____

**h**  What is *Mayo* short for? _____

**i**  What are *Kartoffelpuffer* made from and what do you eat with them?

_____

**j**  What's special about *Glühwein*? _____

**k**  Where in town is the *Innenstadt*? _____

**l**  What makes the kids happy? _____

**Adjective endings**

When an adjective comes in front of a noun, it needs an extra ending.

| Nominative (subject) | | Accusative (object) | |
|---|---|---|---|
| Das ist/sind … | | Ich habe … | |
| *masculine* | ein toll**er** Fußball | *masculine* | ein**en** toll**en** Fußball |
| *feminine* | eine toll**e** CD | *feminine* | eine toll**e** CD |
| *neuter* | ein toll**es** Buch | *neuter* | ein toll**es** Buch |
| *plural* | neu**e** Schuhe | *plural* | neu**e** Schuhe |

**1** **Insert the adjective indicated in brackets, using the right ending.**

Nominative

**a** Ein _____neuer_____ Computer kostet viel Geld. (*new*)

**b** Das ist mein _____ Auto. (*new*)

**c** Das ist ein _____ Film. (*interesting*)

**d** Nena ist eine _____ Sängerin. (*German*)

| masculine | feminine | neuter |
|---|---|---|
| Film | Sängerin | Haus |
| Player | Stadt | Auto |
| Computer | | |

Accusative

**e** Wir haben ein _____ Haus. (*big*)

**f** Leo hat einen _____ Film gesehen. (*old*)

**g** Ich kaufe einen _____ MP3-Player. (*modern*)

**h** In Frankreich haben wir eine _____ Stadt besucht. (*pretty*)

**The future**

To talk about the future, you can use the present tense of *werden* plus the main verb (in the infinitive) at the end of the sentence.

Ich spiele Tennis. (*I play tennis.*) ⟶ Ich **werde** Tennis spielen. (*I will play tennis.*)

**2** **Add the correct part of *werden* to these future tense sentences, and also an infinitive to match the English verb in brackets.**

**a** Wir __werden__ im Winter _____ . (*go skiing*)

**b** Meine Mutter _____ um 22 Uhr nach Hause _____ . (*come*)

**c** Ich _____ eine Bratwurst _____ . (*buy*)

**d** Was _____ du heute Abend _____ ? (*do*)

**e** Leo und Anna _____ Tennis _____ . (*play*)

| ich werde |
|---|
| du wirst |
| er/sie/es wird |
| wir werden |
| ihr werdet |
| sie/Sie werden |

## Pronunciation

**1** Try saying these words out loud. Some of them you haven't seen before but you can still pronounce them.

🎧 Listen to the recording to check and repeat.

| | | | | | |
|---|---|---|---|---|---|
| **a** Wasser | **h** Gewitter | **o** Möwe |
| **b** Wetter | **i** Verein | **p** vielleicht |
| **c** Winter | **j** von | **q** Volker |
| **d** vier | **k** Wagen | **r** Wiebke |
| **e** Viertel | **l** Ingwer | **s** Wannsee |
| **f** Vater | **m** Verden | **t** Vogel |
| **g** warm | **n** Wolle | |

**Remember ...**
- a German **W** sounds like an English **V**
- a German **V** sounds like an English **F**

- You probably haven't come across the last nine words before. Try to work out what they are. You'll have to do some research. (Some are names of places or people.)

## Connectives

**2** Fill in this grid to make a summary of the connectives you have learnt.

| Word | Meaning | Sends verb to end? YES / NO |
|---|---|---|
| weil | because | yes |
| aber | | |
| oder | | |
| denn | | |
| wenn | | |
| und | | |

**3** Make a ridiculously long sentence by adding connectives into all the gaps. It needs to make sense. Read it out, if you have enough breath!

Gestern bin ich in den Supermarkt gegangen, ___weil___ ich Brot kaufen wollte, _____ es gab kein Brot, _____ der Ofen war kaputt _____ der Bäcker war krank, _____ vielleicht war er nicht krank _____ er war nicht da, _____ er faul war _____ das war ein Problem, _____ ich Hunger hatte und _____ ich Hunger habe, bin ich böse!*

*böse – angry*

## Mein Lieblingshobby — *My favourite hobby*

|  |  |
|---|---|
| Was machst du gern/nicht gern? | *What do/don't you like doing?* |
| Ich besuche Freunde. | *I visit friends.* |
| Ich fotografiere. | *I do photography.* |
| Ich höre Musik. | *I listen to music.* |
| Ich lese Bücher. | *I read books.* |
| Ich mache Leichtathletik/ Sport. | *I do athletics/sport.* |
| Ich sammle Karten. | *I collect cards.* |
| Ich sehe fern. | *I watch TV.* |
| Ich singe in einem Chor. | *I sing in a choir.* |
| Ich spiele Theater. | *I'm in a drama group.* |
| Ich surfe im Internet. | *I surf the internet.* |
| Ich tanze. | *I go dancing.* |

| Ich spiele … | *I play …* |
|---|---|
| Computerspiele. | *computer games.* |
| Fußball. | *football.* |
| Gitarre. | *guitar.* |
| Golf. | *golf.* |
| Saxofon. | *saxophone.* |
| Schach. | *chess.* |
| Schlagzeug. | *drums.* |
| Tennis. | *tennis.* |
| Tischtennis. | *table tennis.* |

| Ich fahre … | *I go …* |
|---|---|
| Rad. | *cycling.* |
| Rennrad. | *cycle racing.* |
| Rollschuh. | *roller-skating.* |
| Schlittschuh. | *ice-skating.* |
| Skateboard. | *skateboarding.* |
| Ski. | *skiing.* |
| Wasserski. | *waterskiing.* |

## Das ist ein tolles Hobby! — *That's a great hobby!*

|  |  |
|---|---|
| Mein Hobby ist/sind … | *My hobby is …* |
| Das ist ein tolles Hobby, … | *It's a great hobby, …* |
| Das Hobby macht Spaß, … | *It's a fun hobby, …* |
| weil es billig ist. | *because it's cheap.* |
| weil ich musikalisch/ sportlich bin. | *because I'm musical/sporty.* |
| denn es ist interessant. | *because it's interesting.* |
| denn es ist ungewöhnlich. | *because it's unusual.* |
| aber es ist teuer. | *but it's expensive.* |
| aber ich habe keine Zeit für andere Hobbys. | *but I have no time for other hobbies.* |

## Wenn es heiß ist, … — *When the weather's hot, …*

|  |  |
|---|---|
| Es ist … heiß/ kalt/ sonnig/ warm/ windig | *It's … hot/ cold/ sunny/ warm/ windy* |
| Es friert. | *It's freezing.* |
| Es gewittert. | *It's stormy/There's thunder and lightning.* |
| Es ist neblig. | *It's foggy.* |
| Es regnet. | *It's raining.* |
| Es schneit. | *It's snowing.* |
| im Frühling | *in spring* |
| im Sommer | *in summer* |
| im Herbst | *in autumn* |
| im Winter | *in winter* |

|  |  |
|---|---|
| Wenn es windig ist, gehe ich Windsurfen. | *When it's windy, I go windsurfing* |
| Ich fahre Inliner, wenn es warm ist. | *I go rollerblading when it's warm.* |

## Nächstes Wochenende — *Next weekend*

| Ich werde … | *I will …* |
|---|---|
| spät aufstehen. | *get up late.* |
| Musik hören. | *listen to music.* |
| Fußball spielen. | *play football.* |
| ein Musical singen. | *sing in a musical.* |
| ein Buch lesen. | *read a book.* |
| Inliner fahren. | *go rollerblading.* |
| fernsehen. | *watch TV.* |
| Gitarre spielen. | *play guitar.* |
| schwimmen. | *go swimming.* |

## Checklist

| How well do you think you can do the following? Write a sentence for each one if you can. | I can do this well | I can do this but not very well | I can't do this yet |
|---|---|---|---|
| 1. talk about my favourite hobby | | | |
| 2. talk about what hobbies I do in different kinds of weather | | | |
| 3. talk about what I will do next weekend | | | |
| 4. use regular and irregular verbs in the present tense | | | |
| 5. use the future tense | | | |
| 6. use the correct word order with linking words | | | |

**1** *Körperquiz.* **Use the picture clues to complete the crossword.**

**Waagerecht (across)**

1   2

4   5

6

**Senkrecht (down)**

1   3

4

- Which of the answers is the odd one out, and why?

_____

**2** **Which of these nouns are singular and which are plural? Write S or P next to each.**

**a** Augen _____    **e** Ohr _____    **h** Arme _____

**b** Nase _____    **f** Bein _____    **i** Zahn _____

**c** Beine _____    **g** Körper _____    **j** Fuß _____

**d** Köpfe _____

- For one of those words, either answer would be correct. Which word, and why?

_____

**3** **Possessive adjectives: fill the gaps, using the words in brackets as cues.**

**a** ___Meine___ Augen sind blau. (*my*)

**b** Anja hat _____ Bein gebrochen. (*her*)

**c** _____ Füße sind sehr groß. (*your*)

**d** Pinocchio ist aus Holz. _____ Nase ist lang. (*his*)

**e** Martin ist sportlich. _____ Körper ist muskulös. (*his*)

**f** Gib mir _____ Hand. (*your*)

# 3A.2 Was fehlt dir?

**1** Write captions for the pictures. Check Unit 3A Vokabular if you need help.

a ___Ich habe..._____

b ___Ich..._____

c ___Mein Bein..._____

d _____

e _____

f _____

g _____

h _____

**2** 🎧 *Beim Arzt.* Listen and work out what's wrong with the patient. Write down each problem in English.

She's got: _____

_____

She hasn't got: _____

What's actually wrong with her? _____

**3** *seit* = since / for
Translate these sentences into German, using the present tense and *seit*.

a I have been in Hannover since Wednesday.

___Ich bin seit..._____

b We have been at home for three weeks.

_____

c Udo has been playing football for three years.

_____

d Marina has been ill since Monday.

_____

e I have been waiting here since 9 o'clock.

_____

# 3A.3 Topfit!

**1** **Translate the second half of each sentence (using *um … zu …*) and write it in.**

**a** Leo geht zum Bäcker, _um Brot …_____ . (*in order to buy bread*)

**b** Boris geht ins Restaurant, _____ . (*in order to eat*)

**c** Wir gehen zur Schule, _____ . (*in order to learn*)

**d** Wir spielen Basketball, _____ . (*in order to stay fit*)

**e** Ich kaufe einen Computer, _____ . (*in order to surf the internet*)

**f** Onkel Jochen spart Geld _____ . (*in order to buy a car*)

**2**  **Listen and take notes in English: what does the speaker do, when and what for?**

|   | Activity | When? | What for? |
|---|---|---|---|
| 1 | walks the dog | | |
| 2 | | | |
| 3 | | | |
| 4 | | | |
| 5 | | | |

**3** **Translate these expressions into German.**

**a** twice a week     _zweimal pro …_____

**b** never _____

**c** often _____

**d** sometimes _____

**e** seldom _____

**f** once a month _____

**g** six times a year _____

**h** three times a day _____

# 3A.4 Du bist, was du isst!

**1** Write the food names in German and add *JA* if they are healthy and *NEIN* if not.

| Englisch | Deutsch | gesund? JA / NEIN |
|---|---|---|
| rye bread | Schwarzbrot | |
| chips | | |
| milk | | |
| vegetables | | |
| sausage | | |
| crisps | | |
| sweets | | |
| fruit | | |
| mineral water | | |
| biscuits | | |

**2** 🎧 Listen to six radio adverts and health tips. Answer the questions in English.

**1a** What is it encouraging you to drink? _____

**1b** Why? _____

**2a** Who is speaking? _____

**2b** What is the advice? _____

**2c** Why? _____

**3a** What should you do? _____

**3b** Why? _____

**4a** What is it encouraging you to do? _____

**4b** Why? _____

**5a** Who is giving advice? _____

**5b** What is the advice? _____

**5c** Why? _____

**6a** What is the advice? _____

**6b** Why? _____

• Which adverts offer <u>healthy</u> advice? Write the numbers. _____

**1  a  Sort out the food words listed (right) into the correct grid columns.**

| Gemüse | Obst | Milchprodukte | Fisch | Fleisch |
|--------|------|---------------|-------|---------|
| Brokkoli | | | | |

| | |
|--------|---------|
| Kartoffeln | Butter |
| Lamm | Wurst |
| Sardellen | Brokkoli |
| Käse | Makrele |
| Schinken | Joghurt |
| Aprikosen | Rotkohl |
| Krabben | Äpfel |
| Erdbeeren | |

**b**  Six of those words are not at all like their English equivalent. Which are they?

_____

**c**  There is one serious 'false friend' here. Which word is it and why?

_____

**2  Read the problem page letter and answer. Are the sentences below true (T), false (F) or not mentioned (NM)?**

**a**  Maria doesn't want to go dancing.  ___F___

**b**  Karin used to be overweight.  _____

**c**  Karin drinks lemonade.  _____

**d**  It's OK to drink cola.  _____

**e**  Chips are bad for you.  _____

**f**  You can eat bread and butter.  _____

**g**  Three portions of fruit and vegetables a day are recommended.  _____

**h**  Playing football would help.  _____

**i**  Walking would help.  _____

**j**  Soon Maria's friends will be laughing at her.  _____

**Liebe Karin,**

**ich hoffe, du kannst mir helfen. Ich bin sechzehn und ich bin übergewichtig\*, finde ich. Ich kann nicht schnell laufen oder tanzen und meine Freundinnen machen sich lustig über mich. Was soll ich tun?**

**Maria**

Liebe Maria,

ich verstehe dein Problem sehr gut. Ich war früher auch übergewichtig\*, aber jetzt bin ich schlank und gesund. Es ist immer wichtig, viel Wasser zu trinken. Vergiss Limonade und Cola, diese Getränke sind viel zu süß. Süßigkeiten, Chips und Hamburger sind natürlich auch „out". Alles, was viel Fett und Zucker hat, ist schlecht für deinen Körper.

Es ist wichtig, täglich Schwarzbrot (ohne Butter) zu essen, und auch viel Obst und Gemüse (mindestens drei Portionen pro Tag). Bananen sind besonders gesund und vitaminreich.

Aber ich glaube, Essen ist nicht dein einziges Problem. Du sollst auch mehr Sport machen. Joggen, Tischtennis, sogar spazieren gehen: alles ist wichtig für deine Gesundheit (mindestens 20 Minuten pro Tag).

Bald wirst du mit deinen Freundinnen wieder tanzen gehen, und sie werden nicht mehr über dich lachen, da bin ich sicher!

Karin

\*übergewichtig *overweight*

## 1 Unjumble these sentences.

**a** bin seit krank Montag Ich.

Ich bin ..._____

**b** wohnen Wir seit diesem sechs Jahren in Haus.

_____

**c** Leo Zoom arbeitet seit drei Radio Monaten bei.

_____

**d** sind Campingplatz Irland seit einer Wir Woche auf einem in.

_____

**e** vier Tagen habe Ich seit Grippe.

_____

> **seit**
> The word *seit* means 'since' a specific time or 'for' a period of time. In English, complicated tenses are used ('I have been living here for …'). In German, it's much simpler – just use the present tense.

## 2 Change these orders into the polite or the familiar imperative form, i.e. if they use *du*, change it to *Sie*, or the other way round.

**a** Steh auf! Stehen ..._____

**b** Kommen Sie mit! _____

**c** Sprich Deutsch! _____

**d** Sag, was du willst! _____

**e** Bleiben Sie hier! _____

**f** Kaufen Sie Hammis Hamburger! _____

> **The imperative**
> If you want to tell someone what to do or give a command in German, you use the imperative form:
> (*du* form) **Trink** mehr Wasser. *Drink more water.*
> (*Sie* form) **Trinken Sie** mehr Wasser. *Drink more water.*

> **um … zu …**
> Use *um … zu …* to say why you do something. It means 'in order to …'
> Put *um* at the beginning of the second clause (after the comma), and put *zu* at the end followed by an infinitive:
> Wir machen oft Sport, **um** fit **zu bleiben**. *We often do sport, to stay fit.*

## 3 Make up your own ending to each sentence, using *um … zu …*

**a** Wir gehen ins Kino, _____ .

**b** Anne nimmt den Bus, _____ .

**c** Oma geht zur Post, _____ .

**d** Wir gehen ins Konzert, _____ .

**e** Ich gehe jetzt ins Bett, _____ .

**f** Ich jogge, _____ .

## Adapting language

**1** **Use patterns learnt in this unit to make new sentences.**

Pattern 1: Ich habe Bauchschmerzen.
Write three more sentences about aches and pains.

_____

_____

_____

Pattern 2: Mein Bein tut weh.
Write three more sentences about things that hurt.

_____

_____

_____

Pattern 3: Ich bin seit einer Stunde hier.
Write three more sentences about how long you have been somewhere.

_____

_____

_____

Pattern 4: Ich spiele Golf, um fit zu bleiben.
Write three sentences about things you do to stay healthy or slim.

_____

_____

_____

Pattern 5: Trink Limonade!
Write three more slogans for unhealthy food or drink.

_____

_____

_____

Pattern 6: Trinken Sie Limonade!
Now do it again, using the polite form.

_____

_____

_____

Pattern 7: Ich esse dreimal pro Tag Gemüse.
Write three more sentences about how often you do things.

_____

_____

> Here are some expressions to help you, but feel free to choose your own.
>
> | | |
> |---|---|
> | Bauch | ich mache ... |
> | Bein | Cola |
> | Fuß | Pommes |
> | Kopf | Chips |
> | Hals | Bonbons |
> | Rücken | Hamburger |
> | Arm | oft |
> | Hand | immer |
> | ich spiele ... | nie |
> | ich esse ... | manchmal |
> | einmal/zweimal/dreimal |
> | pro Stunde/Tag/Monat |
> | seit einer Stunde |
> | seit einer Woche |
> | seit drei Tagen |

> Aim for better marks by adding other information and vocabulary, as long as you are reasonably confident it is correct. For example, express opinions by adding adjectives, or give reasons, using *weil*.

## Der Körper — The body

| der Arm (-e) | arm |
|---|---|
| das Auge (-n) | eye |
| das Bein (-e) | leg |
| der Finger (-) | finger |
| der Fuß (Füße) | foot |
| die Hand (Hände) | hand |
| das Knie (-) | knee |
| der Kopf (Köpfe) | head |
| der Körper (-) | body |
| der Mund (Münder) | mouth |
| die Nase (-n) | nose |
| das Ohr (-en) | ear |
| der Zahn (Zähne) | tooth |

## Was fehlt dir? — What's wrong?

| Ich habe … | I have … |
|---|---|
| Bauchschmerzen | stomach ache |
| Halsschmerzen | a sore throat |
| Knieschmerzen | a sore knee |
| Kopfschmerzen | a headache |
| Ohrenschmerzen | earache |
| Rückenschmerzen | backache |
| Zahnschmerzen | toothache |
| Fieber | a fever, a high temperature |
| eine Grippe | flu |
| Wie geht es dir? | How are you? |
| Es geht mir (nicht) gut. | I'm (not) well. |
| Ich bin krank. | I'm ill. |
| Mein Bein tut weh. | My leg hurts. |
| Ich habe mir die Nase gebrochen. | I've broken my nose. |
| Ich habe eine Allergie gegen Katzen. | I'm allergic to cats. |
| Ich habe Migräne. | I've got a migraine. |
| seit einer Woche/vier Tagen | for a week/four days |
| Es tut mir leid. | I'm sorry. |

## Topfit! — Superfit!

| Ich mache … | I do … |
|---|---|
| Karate/Pilates. | karate/Pilates. |
| Sport/Yoga. | sport/yoga. |
| Ich spiele … | I play … |
| Basketball. | basketball. |
| Tischtennis. | table tennis. |
| Volleyball. | volleyball. |
| Ich jogge. | I go jogging. |
| Ich gehe (mit dem Hund) spazieren. | I go walking (with the dog). |
| Ich gehe zu Fuß in die Schule. | I walk to school. |
| Ich mache Sport, um fit zu bleiben. | I do sport in order to keep fit. |
| hin und wieder | now and then |

| manchmal | sometimes |
|---|---|
| nie | never |
| oft | often |
| selten | seldom |
| einmal/zweimal pro Woche | once/twice a week |
| dreimal pro Monat | three times a month |

## Du bist, was du isst! — You are what you eat!

| die Chips | crisps |
|---|---|
| die Cola | cola |
| das Eis | ice cream |
| das Fastfood | fast food |
| das Gemüse | vegetables |
| der Käse | cheese |
| die Kekse | biscuits, cookies |
| die Milch | milk |
| das Obst | fruit |
| die Pommes | chips |
| die Süßigkeiten | sweets |
| das Mineralwasser | mineral water |
| das Schwarzbrot | rye bread |
| das Weißbrot | white bread |
| die Wurst | sausage |

| Ich esse normalerweise/oft/selten/nie … | I usually/often/rarely/never eat … |
|---|---|
| Iss kein Fastfood! | Don't eat fast food! |
| Trinken Sie viel Wasser! | Drink lots of water! |

## Checklist

| How well do you think you can do the following? | | | |
|---|---|---|---|
| Write a sentence for each one if you can. | | | |
| | I can do this well | I can do this but not very well | I can't do this yet |
| 1. name parts of the body | | | |
| 2. talk about illness and injuries | | | |
| 3. talk about what sports I do to keep fit | | | |
| 4. talk about healthy eating | | | |
| 5. use possessive adjectives | | | |
| 6. use seit | | | |

**1** Complete the sentences with phrases from the box. Use your powers of logic!

a Wir haben Hunger. Wir brauchen _____

b Wir wollen schlafen. Wir brauchen _____

c Hotels sind zu teuer. Wir brauchen _____

d Campingplätze sind zu kalt. Wir brauchen _____

e Aber wo ist die Jugendherberge? Wir brauchen _____

f Wir müssen mit dem Bus fahren. Wir brauchen _____

g Wir wissen nichts über Düsseldorf. Wir brauchen _____

> eine Broschüre über die Stadt
> eine Liste von Hotels
> eine Liste von Jugendherbergen
> einen Stadtplan
> einen Fahrplan
> eine Liste von Campingplätzen
> eine Liste von Restaurants

**2** Read this letter to a tourist information office. Find the German equivalent for phrases a–i below. Some may be new to you but they are easy to guess.

Sehr geehrte Damen und Herren,

wir werden im Oktober nach Münster fahren, denn wir haben gehört, dass die Stadt besonders schön ist. Können Sie bitte ein paar Fragen beantworten?

Wir sind vier Personen, ich, meine Frau und unsere zwei Kinder (8 und 6 Jahre). Hotels sind leider zu teuer für uns. Gibt es vielleicht eine Jugendherberge in der Stadt?

Was gibt es in Münster zu sehen und zu tun? Vergessen Sie bitte nicht, dass die Kinder noch klein sind und sich nicht für Museen und Kunstgalerien interessieren. Gibt es einen Park und vielleicht einen Zoo?

Wir möchten gern eine Broschüre über die Sehenswürdigkeiten und auch, wenn möglich, eine Liste von Restaurants. Natürlich brauchen wir auch einen Stadtplan.

Vielen Dank im Voraus.

Mit freundlichen Grüßen,

Axel Müller

a we have heard: _wir haben gehört_

b particularly nice: _____

c a few: _____

d unfortunately: _____

e perhaps: _____

f art gallery: _____

g if possible: _____

h of course: _____

i in advance: _____

• Explain why *ein paar* is a false friend. _____

**3** On separate paper, write a similar letter to a tourist office in a different town. Change the enquiries if you like. Use some of the phrases from Activity 2 to make your letter sound as natural as possible.

# 3B.2 Was kann man machen?

**1** 🎧 **Listen and answer the questions in German.**

**a** Ist Zürich in Deutschland?

Nein (in der Schweiz)

**b** Was kann man in der Bahnhofsstraße machen?

_____

**c** Was ist das Problem mit den Geschäften?

_____

**d** Sind die Hotels preiswert?

_____

**e** Wo ist die beste Jugendherberge?

_____

**f** Wo kann man spazieren gehen?

_____

**g** Was kann man im 'El Lokal' machen?

_____

**2** **Agree to go to these places, following the example.**

**a** Monika ist im Park. Gut, gehen wir in den Park.

**b** Es gibt einen guten Film im Kino. Gut, _____

**c** Das Museum ist interessant. Gut, _____

**d** Die Disco ist toll. Gut, _____

**e** Man kann in der Bahnhofstraße gut einkaufen. Gut, _____

**f** Es gibt Elefanten im Zoo. Gut, _____

> **Remember the genders:**
> • der Zoo / Film / Park
> • die Straße / Disco
> • das Kino

**3** **Make a list of things people can do in your town. Use vocabulary you know from this module and look up any extra words you need. Mention at least five things. Add further information and comments if you can.**

Man kann ...

_____

_____

_____

_____

_____

**1** 🎧 **Listen to identify the places on the map and write them in.**

✗ | Du bist hier

**2** 🎧 **Listen again. What other information does each speaker give?**

1 _____    4 _____

2 _____    5 _____

3 _____    6 _____

**3** **Study the train journey information (right) and answer the questions.**

**a** Is this a single or return ticket? Journey 1: _____ Journey 2: _____

**b** What class is it in? Journey 1: _____ Journey 2: _____

**c** Does the passenger have to change? Journey 1: _____ Journey 2: _____

1

Hamburg–Oldenburg
(hin und zurück)

Direkt | Hin: | Gleis 4, 9:30 Uhr

Zurück: | Gleis 4, 14:22 Uhr

€ | Preis: €27,50

**4** **Make up dialogues with a partner.**

**a** Make a street map like the one in Activity 1. Direct your partner to places of your choice. Check that he/she has got them right.

Example: **A** *Geh geradeaus und nimm die erste Straße rechts.*
         **B** *Ist das der Bahnhof?*
         **A** *Ja, richtig!*

**b** Make up two dialogues at the station ticket counter, where the traveller buys a ticket for each journey in Activity 2.

Example: **A** *Wann fährt der Zug nach Oldenburg, bitte?*
         **B** *Um neun Uhr dreißig.*
         **A** *Eine Fahrkarte bitte, hin und zurück, erste Klasse.*
         **B** *Ja, das kostet 27 Euro 50.*
         **A** *Wo fährt der Zug ab?*
         **B** *Von Gleis 4.*

2

Frankfurt–Stuttgart
(über Mannheim, einfache Fahrt)

2 Kl. | Gleis 3, 16:46 Uhr

€ | Preis: €33,30

**1** Complete the sentences with prepositions and nouns, describing where the items are.

**masculine:** Tisch / Stuhl
**feminine:** Tür / Pflanze

**a** Der Computer ist _auf dem Tisch._

**b** Die Katze ist _____

**c** Das Buch ist _____

**d** Die Schuhe sind _____

**e** Die Pflanze ist _____

**f** Der Rucksack ist _____

**2** Complete these perfect tense sentences with the appropriate forms of *haben* or *sein* and the past participles.

**a** Wir ___haben___ einen neuen Computer _____ . *(bought)*

**b** _____ du den Film _____ ? *(seen)*

**c** Emma _____ im Meer _____ . *(swum)*

**d** Ich _____ bis drei Uhr morgens _____ . *(danced)*

**e** Oma und Opa _____ das Schloss _____ . *(visited)*

**f** Wir _____ in einem griechischen Restaurant _____ . *(eaten)*

**g** Ali _____ mit dem Rad _____ . *(gone)*

**h** Er _____ um acht Uhr _____ . *(got up)*

**i** Ich _____ noch nie Cola _____ . *(drunk)*

**j** Na, was _____ du _____ ? *(done)*

**3** Look around you. Describe where some things are in your room or classroom. Use *auf, in, unter, neben, vor, hinter* or *zwischen* and *dem* with masculine and neuter nouns, *der* with feminine ones.

_____

_____

_____

_____

_____

_____

### Kronberg

**Kronberg im Taunus grüßt Sie!**

**Attraktionen:** Das Schloss ist morgens und nachmittags für Besucher geöffnet, von 9 Uhr bis 12 Uhr 30 und von 14 Uhr 30 bis 18 Uhr. Eintritt: Erwachsene €3, Kinder €1. Das Schloss-Restaurant ist momentan wegen Renovierungsarbeiten* geschlossen.

Der Golfplatz ist täglich von 7 Uhr bis 20 Uhr geöffnet. Besucher sind willkommen (nur Erwachsene).

Das öffentliche Freibad ist von Mai bis Oktober geöffnet. Eintritt: Erwachsene €5, Kinder €2. Der Freibad-Imbiss bietet Bockwurst mit Kartoffelsalat.

In der Stadtmitte befinden sich mehrere Einkaufsstraßen. Hier findet man schicke Boutiquen, nette Restaurants und Lokale, Supermärkte und Souvenirläden. In der Regel sind alle Geschäfte mittags geschlossen.

Kronberg ist von einem herrlichen Wald umgeben. Hier kann man wandern oder Mountainbike fahren.

Weitere Informationen erhalten Sie im Informationsbüro, Katharinenstraße 7.

*Renovierungsarbeiten – *renovation work*

**1** **Read the web page about Kronberg.** *Richtig oder falsch?*
**For sentences a–j, put R if the sentence is *richtig* and F if it is *falsch*.**

**a** Man kann um 13 Uhr das Schloss besichtigen. ☐ F

**b** Man kann im Schloss essen. ☐

**c** Kinder dürfen Golf spielen. ☐

**d** Man kann in Mai schwimmen gehen. ☐

**e** Im Freibad-Imbiss kann man Pommes kaufen. ☐

**f** In Kronberg kann man gut einkaufen. ☐

**g** Man kann um 15 Uhr Souvenirs kaufen. ☐

**h** In der Nähe von Kronberg kann man wandern. ☐

**i** Mountainbike fahren ist verboten. ☐

**j** Man kann online mehr Informationen finden. ☐

**2** **For any sentences you identified as *falsch*, explain why (in English): add notes next to the sentences above.**

These prepositions are always followed by the **dative** (m. *dem*, f. *der*, n. *dem*):
**seit  zu  nach  von  mit  aus**
Remember that *zu dem* is shortened to *zum*.

These prepositions are followed by the **dative** (m. *dem*, f. *der*, n. *dem*) if there is <u>no</u> movement and the **accusative** (m. *den*, f. *die*, n. *das*) if there <u>is</u> movement:
**in  auf  hinter  neben  vor  unter  zwischen**
Remember that *in dem* is shortened to *im* and *in das* is shortened to *ins*.

**1** 🎧 **Listen carefully: are the speakers talking about where they <u>are</u> or where they <u>are going</u>?**

1 (are) / are going

2 are / are going

3 are / are going

4 are / are going

5 are / are going

6 are / are going

**2** **Fill in the gaps with *den, die, das, der* or *dem*.**

**a** Wir fahren mit ____dem____ Bus.

**b** Wir sind seit _____ Sommer hier.

**c** Gehst du in _____ Schule?

**d** Sira kocht in _____ Küche einen Kaffee.

**e** Jens kommt morgen aus _____ Krankenhaus.

**f** Leg das Buch auf _____ Tisch.

**g** Das Restaurant ist neben _____ Bäckerei.

**h** Was machst du nach _____ Schule?

**i** Wir kommen aus _____ Schweiz.

**j** Leo legt das Buch auf _____ Regal.

| masculine | feminine | neuter |
|-----------|----------|--------|
| Bus | Schule | Krankenhaus |
| Sommer | Bäckerei | Sportzentrum |
| Tisch | Schweiz | Regal |
|  | Küche |  |

# 3B.6B Think

## Reading different text styles

**1** Read the text extracts, decide which category they belong to, and write the letter of each extract in the right places.

Instructions: _____

Formal letter: _____

Informal letter: _____

Book/Literary text: _____

Newspaper article: _____

Magazine article: _____

(a)
> Hallo Ahmed!
>
> Hast du Lust, am Wochenende ins Hallenbad zu gehen?
>
> Pinar

(b) Können Sie uns bitte eine Broschüre schicken?

(c) **Bitte den Rasen nicht betreten!**

(d) Rotkäppchen hat den Wolf gesehen und hatte Angst.

(e) Nächste Woche in Top-Teen: **Ein tolles INTERVIEW mit Sebastian Vettel**

(f) In der Innenstadt hat man am Freitag in ein Juweliergeschäft eingebrochen.

## Working out missing words

**2** Use your powers of logic to fill in the gaps. Only one word suits each gap. The words are given below in English, but you need the German word. Watch out for grammatical traps!

Sira und ich sind am letzten __Samstag__ mit _____ Bus nach

Kronberg _____. Zuerst sind wir _____ Schloss gegangen.

Es war _____ schön, aber ein bisschen _____. Wir hatten

_____, aber das Restaurant war _____. Am _____

sind wir einkaufen _____. Die Geschäfte _____ langweilig,

absolut nichts für _____ Leute. Also sind wir in den _____

gegangen. Das Wandern hat _____ gemacht, aber am Abend waren

wir _____ müde.

| | | | | |
|---|---|---|---|---|
| fun | travelled | hunger | Saturday | the |
| the | to the | were | quite | closed |
| old-fashioned | young | gone | afternoon | very |

## Wir brauchen Infos!
## We need info!

| | |
|---|---|
| Wir brauchen … | We need … |
| eine Broschüre über die Stadt. | a brochure about the town. |
| einen Fahrplan. | a timetable. |
| eine Liste von billigen Hotels/Restaurants. | a list of cheap hotels/restaurants. |
| eine Liste von Campingplätzen/Jugendherbergen. | a list of campsites/youth hostels. |
| einen Stadtplan. | a map of the town. |

## Was kann man machen?
## What can you do?

| | |
|---|---|
| Man kann/Wir können … | You/We can … |
| einen Einkaufsbummel machen. | go on a shopping expedition. |
| das Filmmuseum besuchen. | visit the Film Museum. |
| den Rheinturm besichtigen. | visit the Rhine Tower. |
| eine Stadtrundfahrt machen. | do a tour of the town. |
| in den Südpark gehen. | go to the South Park. |

## Zwei Fahrkarten, bitte!
## Two tickets, please!

| | |
|---|---|
| Wie komme ich am besten … | What's the best way … |
| zum Bahnhof? | to the railway station? |
| zur nächsten U-Bahn-Station? | to the nearest underground station? |
| zum Kino? | to the cinema? |
| Wo ist die nächste … | Where's the nearest … |
| Bushaltestelle? | bus stop? |
| S-Bahn-Station? | S-Bahn station? |
| Geh/Gehen Sie … | Go … |
| Nimm/Nehmen Sie … | Take … |
| links/rechts/geradeaus | left/right/straight on |
| die erste Straße rechts | the first road on the right |
| die zweite Straße links | the second road on the left |
| über die Brücke | over the bridge |
| an der Ampel/Kreuzung | at the traffic lights/crossroads |

| | |
|---|---|
| Ich möchte zwei Fahrkarten nach …, bitte. | I'd like two tickets to …, please. |
| Einfach oder hin und zurück? | One-way or return? |
| Erster oder zweiter Klasse? | First or second class? |
| Was kosten die Fahrkarten? | How much are the tickets? |
| Eine Fahrkarte kostet … Euro. | One ticket costs … euros. |
| Fährt der Zug direkt? | Is this a direct train? |
| Nein, Sie müssen in … umsteigen. | No, you have to change in … |
| Wann fährt der Zug ab? | When does the train leave? |
| Und wann kommt er an? | When does it arrive? |
| Die Fahrt wird … Minuten dauern. | The journey will take … minutes. |

## Wieder zu Hause!
## Home again!

| | |
|---|---|
| das Hemd | shirt |
| die Jacke | jacket |
| der Kapuzenpullover | hooded jumper |
| der Pullover | jumper |
| die Schuhe | shoes |
| | |
| unter dem Bett | under the bed |
| neben dem Computer | next to the computer |
| auf dem Regal | on the shelf |
| zwischen dem Bett und dem Stuhl | between the bed and the chair |
| vor dem Schreibtisch | in front of the desk |
| an der Tür | on the door |
| im Schrank | in the wardrobe |
| hinter dem Bett | behind the bed |
| | |
| Wir sind … | We … |
| gefahren/gegangen/angekommen/geschwommen. | travelled/went/arrived/swam … |
| Wir haben … | We … |
| besichtigt/besucht. | visited … |
| gekauft/gespielt. | bought/played … |
| gesehen/gemacht. | saw/did … |
| getanzt. | danced. |
| gegessen/getrunken. | ate/drank … |

## Checklist

| How well do you think you can do the following? | | | |
|---|---|---|---|
| Write a sentence for each one if you can. | | | |
| | I can do this well | I can do this but not very well | I can't do this yet |
| 1. plan a trip and write a formal letter | | | |
| 2. say what there is to see and do in a town | | | |
| 3. ask for directions and buy train tickets | | | |
| 4. say where things are in a room | | | |
| 5. describe a trip using past tenses | | | |
| 6. identify different styles of writing | | | |

# 4A.1 Meine Gegend

**1** **Find the matching German words and fill them in. What is the mystery word (in the tinted box down)?**

1 coast

2 large city

3 port in northern Germany

4 village

5 small town

6 in the mountains = *in den ...*

7 country

8 Germany's capital

9 town

Mystery word: _____

**2** 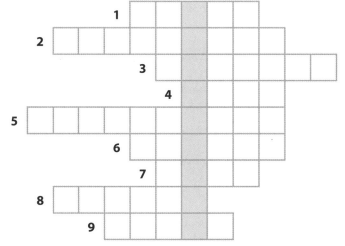 **Listen to the six people and, in each case, write:**

- where the person lives
- what the person thinks of it
- why. Give details if you can.

1 _____

_____

2 _____

_____

3 _____

_____

4 _____

_____

5 _____

_____

6 _____

_____

**1** Unjumble the words for forms of transport. Write the words in the boxes. Then draw lines to link the boxes to the correct pictures.

ARAFHRD  [ ]

GUZ  [ ]

SUB  [ ]

RßATSNEHNAB  [ ]

ADOOMTRR  [ ]

ZULGFUEG  [ ]

OTUA  [ ]

**2** Write in the correct definite article.

**a** Wir fahren mit ____der____ U-Bahn in die Stadt.

**b** Ich fahre mit _____ Bus zur Schule.

**c** Papa fährt mit _____ Auto in den Urlaub.

**d** Man fährt mit _____ Straßenbahn zum Krankenhaus.

**e** Wir fliegen mit _____ Flugzeug nach New York.

**f** Die Hells Angels fahren mit _____ Motorrad.

| masculine | feminine | neuter |
|-----------|----------|--------|
| Bus | U-Bahn | Auto |
| | Straßenbahn | Flugzeug |
| | | Motorrad |

**3** Use the expressions in the box below to write three sentences saying <u>where</u> you go, <u>when</u> and <u>by what means of transport.</u> Remember the correct order in German: time, manner, place. Feel free to use your own ideas, not just these ones.

_____

_____

_____

| ich fahre | am Montag | mit dem Rad | in die Stadt |
|-----------|-----------|-------------|--------------|
| | jeden Tag | mit dem Auto | zur Schule |
| | am Wochenende | mit der Bahn | nach Hannover |

# 4A.3 Umweltschutz

**Umfrage: Bist du umweltfreundlich?**

**1** Find out how much your classmates care about the environment.
First, translate these questions into German.

1 Do you often go on foot?    Gehst du ..._____

2 Do you separate the rubbish?    _____

3 Do you take glass bottles to the bottle bank? ·_____

4 Do you use plastic bags?    _____

5 Do you shower or bathe?    _____

6 Do you save electricity?    _____

**2** Ask at least ten people in your class questions 1–6 (above) in German.
Tick *Ja* or *Nein* to record their answers in the grid.

| Question | Ja | Nein |
|---|---|---|
| 1 | | |
| 2 | | |
| 3 | | |
| 4 | | |
| 5 | | |
| 6 | | |

**3** Fill the gaps in this summary of your survey results. (Watch out – the
actions are listed in a different order.)

_____ people separate their rubbish.          _____ people go to the bottle bank.

_____ people take showers rather than baths.   _____ people don't use plastic bags.

_____ people save electricity.                 _____ people often walk.

**4** 🎧 Listen: is each person eco-friendly or not? Tick *umweltfreundlich* or
*umweltfeindlich*.

1 umweltfreundlich ☐    umweltfeindlich ☐    _____

2 umweltfreundlich ☐    umweltfeindlich ☐    _____

3 umweltfreundlich ☐    umweltfeindlich ☐    _____

4 umweltfreundlich ☐    umweltfeindlich ☐    _____

5 umweltfreundlich ☐    umweltfeindlich ☐    _____

● **In English, give a reason for your answer in each case.**

**1** *Umweltquiz.* **Find ten words about the environment in this grid. They can be down, across or diagonal. The words are provided below in English. You need the German words!**

| O | A | K | R | A | U | M | W | E | L | T | P |
|---|---|---|---|---|---|---|---|---|---|---|---|
| I | Z | P | U | E | Z | N | N | N | I | M | U |
| N | H | O | K | Ö | J | Ü | E | T | F | Ü | M |
| D | ß | L | N | W | T | I | P | W | W | L | V |
| U | M | Ü | A | L | G | E | R | A | T | L | E |
| S | Ü | S | T | R | O | G | R | L | D | B | R |
| T | L | Ä | E | F | Ä | C | Z | D | A | E | K |
| R | T | N | A | T | U | R | H | U | Ü | R | E |
| I | E | G | S | T | R | O | M | N | J | G | H |
| E | X | K | L | I | M | A | Z | G | O | Z | R |

hole in the ozone layer
mountain of rubbish
energy
environment
traffic
climate
electricity
industry
deforestation
nature

**2** **Fill the gaps with the German adjective and the matching comparative and superlative forms.**

**a** Die Müllberge sind _____schlimm_____ *(bad)*, der Verkehr ist _____ *(worse)*, aber das Ozonloch ist _____ *(worst)*.

**b** Duschen ist _____ *(good)*, zu Fuß gehen ist _____ *(better)*, aber Recycling ist _____ *(best)*.

**c** Die Luftverschmutzung ist ein _____ *(big)* Problem, der Atommüll ist ein _____ *(bigger)* Problem, aber das _____ *(biggest)* Problem ist der Klimawandel.

**3** **Which of these words are made up of two or more words put together? When you have found them, split them into their components and try to work out what they mean.**

**a** **Treibhauseffekt** _____

**b** **Müllberg** _____

**c** **Natur** _____

**d** **Pflanze** _____

**e** **Ozonloch** _____

**f** **Wald** _____

**g** **Verkehr** _____

**h** **Klimawandel** _____

**1** 🎧 **Listen to this conversation between grandfather and grandson. Answer the questions in English, giving as much detail as you can.**

**a** What's the first thing Peter says about his school?

_____

**b** Why is it warm in winter?

_____

**c** What does his grandfather say about the temperature in his school?

_____

**d** What does Peter say about recycling in his school?

_____

**e** What unbelievable thing does his grandfather say?

_____

**f** What does Peter say about the school garden?

_____

**g** Guess what *Beton* means.

_____

**h** What conclusion does Peter's grandfather reach?

_____

**2** **Read these sentences and decide whether they refer to past, present or future.**

**a** Alles war schmutzig. _____

**b** Schulen werden umweltfreundlich sein. _____

**c** Wir haben vier Müllcontainer. _____

**d** Wir hatten keine Pflanzen. _____

**e** Unsere Schule ist sehr sauber. _____

**f** Wir werden energiesparende Computer haben. _____

**1** **Complete each sentence with the right ending from the box on the right, translated into German.**

**a** Es ist schön ruhig, _____

**b** Ich bin umweltfreundlich, _____

**c** Hier ist es stressig, _____

**d** Die Luft ist schlecht, _____

**e** Ich musste eine Plastiktüte kaufen, _____

**f** Ich gehe zu Fuß in die Stadt, _____

> **weil** ('because')
> The word *weil* has a comma before it and sends the verb to the end.

**2** **Write in *der* or *dem*.**

**a** Ich fahre oft mit ___dem___ Rad.

**b** Wir fahren nie mit _____ Auto.

**c** Fährst du mit _____ Straßenbahn?

**d** Opa fährt mit _____ U-Bahn.

**e** Oma fährt mit _____ Bus.

**These three use a shortened form:**

**f** Wie komme ich _____ Krankenhaus?

**g** Ich fahre _____ Arbeit.

**h** Wir gehen _____ Bäckerei.

> *because it is noisy*
> *because I forgot my cloth bag*
> *because I always recycle*
> *because it is healthy*
> *because there is so much traffic*
> *because we live in a village*

> **Comparative and superlative**
>
> For the comparative, add *-er* to the adjective:
> toll ⟶ toll**er** (*great, greater*)   schlecht ⟶ schlecht**er** (*bad, worse*)
>
> For some short adjectives, add an umlaut to the first vowel:
> alt ⟶ **ä**lt**er** (*old, older*)
>
> Some comparatives are irregular and have a different word altogether:
> gut ⟶ besser (*good, better*)
>
> For the superlative of regular adjectives, add *am* before the adjective and *-sten* or *-esten* to the end:
> schlimm ⟶ **am** schlimm**sten** (*bad, worst*)

> **The dative**
> After prepositions like *mit* and *zu*, the dative form is used (m: *dem*, f: *der*, n: *dem*). *Zu der* is shortened to *zur* and *zu dem* to *zum*.

**3** **Fill in the comparative and superlative adjectives.**

**a** Eine Kuh ist _____ als eine Maus, aber ein
Elefant ist am _____ . (*big*)

**b** Ein Audi ist _____ als ein VW, aber ein
Mercedes ist am _____ . (*expensive*)

**c** Reggae ist _____ als klassische Musik, aber
Heavy Metal ist am _____ . (*loud*)

## Checking your written work

**1** **Translate these simple sentences, keeping the spelling tips in mind.**

    **a** My dog runs fast. _____

    **b** I have a nice bike. _____

    **c** We write a lot of letters. _____

    **d** How many sausages have you eaten? _____

    **e** I would like to go home. _____

    **f** How far is Munich? _____

> **Spelling**
> Put a capital letter at the start of each noun. Remember umlauts! Check you haven't got **ei** and **ie** mixed up: saying the word out loud can help. Check you have put **sch** and not **sh**.

> **Tenses**
> If it's present tense, remember it may be an irregular verb.
> If it's perfect tense, use *haben* or *sein* plus the past participle at the end.
> If it's future tense, use *werden* plus the infinitive at the end.

**2** **Translate these simple sentences into German.**

    **a** He travels by car.     Er fährt … _____

    **b** He travelled by car. _____

    **c** He will travel by car. _____

    **d** We use plastic bags. _____

    **e** We used plastic bags. _____

    **f** We will use plastic bags. _____

    **g** Do you smoke? *(du)* _____

    **h** Did you smoke? _____

    **i** Will you smoke? _____

**3** **Translate these sentences.**

    **a** We will travel to Bonn by bus on Friday.

    _____

    **b** I live with my mother in the country.

    _____

    **c** Leo has worked with his friends at Radio Zoom for six months.

    _____

> **Word order**
> Check that you have followed the rules: verb second, then time, manner, place.

| Meine Gegend | My area |
|---|---|
| Ich wohne … | I live … |
| in einem Dorf | in a village |
| in einer Stadt/Großstadt | in a town/city |
| in einer Industriestadt | in an industrial town |
| in einer Kleinstadt | in a small town |
| am Stadtrand | in the suburbs |
| an der Küste | by the coast |
| auf dem Land | in the country |
| in den Bergen | in the mountains |
| Ich wohne (nicht) gern hier, weil … | I (don't) like living here because … |
| es viel Kriminalität gibt. | there's a lot of crime. |
| es zu viele Autos gibt. | there are too many cars. |
| es nichts für Jugendliche gibt. | there's nothing for young people. |
| man viel machen kann. | you can do lots, there's lots to do. |
| es … ist. | it's … |
| langweilig | boring |
| laut | noisy |
| praktisch | practical |
| ruhig | quiet |
| sauber | clean |
| schmutzig | dirty |
| schön | nice, beautiful |
| sicher | safe |

| Bus und Bahn | By bus and rail |
|---|---|
| Ich fahre mit … | I go/travel by … |
| dem Auto/Bus/Zug. | car/bus/train. |
| dem Fahrrad/Motorrad. | bike/motorbike. |
| der U-Bahn/Straßenbahn. | underground/tram. |
| Ich fliege mit dem Flugzeug. | I fly by plane. |
| Ich gehe zu Fuß. | I walk/go on foot. |
| zum Flughafen | to the airport |
| zur Schule/Arbeit | to school/work |
| zum Kino | to the cinema |
| nach Frankreich | to France |
| in den Urlaub | on holiday |

| Umweltschutz | Protecting the environment |
|---|---|
| Ich spare Strom. | I save electricity. |
| Ich nehme keine Plastiktüten, sondern Stofftaschen. | I don't take plastic bags, I take cloth bags. |
| Meine Familie nutzt … | My family uses … |
| alternative Energien. | alternative energy. |
| Sonnen-/Windenergie. | solar/wind energy. |
| Ich dusche/Ich bade nicht. | I shower/I don't have a bath. |
| Wir haben drei Mülleimer. | We have three bins. |
| Wir trennen unseren Müll. | We separate our litter. |
| Ich recycle Papier/Dosen. | I recycle paper/cans. |
| Ich bringe Glasflaschen zum Container. | I take glass bottles to the bottle bank. |

| Ich habe … | I … |
|---|---|
| gebadet/geduscht. | bathed/showered. |
| … gebracht/genommen. | brought/took … |
| … genutzt/gespart. | used/saved … |
| … getrennt/recycelt. | separated/recycled … |
| Ich bin … gegangen/gefahren. | I went/travelled … |
| Ich werde … | I will … |
| baden/duschen. | bathe/shower. |
| … bringen/nehmen. | bring/take … |
| … nutzen/sparen. | use/save … |
| … trennen/recyceln. | separate/recycle … |
| … gehen/fahren. | go/travel … |

| Fünf vor zwölf | Five to twelve |
|---|---|
| der Atommüll | nuclear waste |
| das Aussterben von Tieren | extinction of animals |
| die Entwaldung | deforestation |
| der Klimawandel | climate change |
| die Luftverschmutzung | air pollution |
| die Müllberge | rubbish mountains |
| das Ozonloch | hole in the ozone layer |
| der Treibhauseffekt | greenhouse effect |
| viel Verkehr | a lot of traffic |

| Man muss … | We must … |
|---|---|
| mehr zu Fuß gehen. | walk more. |

## Checklist

| How well do you think you can do the following? | | | |
|---|---|---|---|
| Write a sentence for each one if you can. | | | |
| | I can do this well | I can do this but not very well | I can't do this yet |
| 1. describe where I live and give my opinion of it | | | |
| 2. talk about ways to travel | | | |
| 3. talk about ways to be environmentally friendly | | | |
| 4. talk about environmental problems and solutions | | | |
| 5. use linking word *weil* | | | |
| 6. use the comparative and the superlative | | | |

**1** **Complete the sentences about part-time jobs.**

**a** Ich führe ___Hunde aus___ . (*dog walking*)

**b** Ich helfe _____ . (*at home*)

**c** Ich gebe _____ . (*tuition*)

**d** Ich wasche _____ . (*cars*)

**e** Ich arbeite _____ . (*in the garden*)

**f** Ich mache _____ . (*babysitting*)

**g** Ich trage _____ . (*paper round*)

**2** 🎧 **Listen and fill in the details: job, opinion, money.**

**1** Sven works in ___a shop___ . It's _____ and

he earns _____ .

**2** Anja earns money by _____ . She thinks it's

_____ but she gets _____ .

**3** Martin works in _____ . The work is

_____ but he earns _____ .

**4** Arno thinks his job is _____ . He delivers

_____ and earns _____ .

**5** Susanne earns money by _____ . She earns

_____ but it's quite _____ .

**3** 🎧 **Listen again and note down, in English, one extra piece of information for each person.**

**1** _____

**2** _____

**3** _____

**4** _____

**5** _____

**1** *Richtig oder falsch?* **For each sentence, circle *R* if it is *richtig* and *F* if it is *falsch*.**

> To revise what you've learnt about German schools, see page 135 of your Student Book.

a In Großbritannien beginnt der Unterricht um acht Uhr.   **R / F**

b In Deutschland geht man oft um 13 Uhr nach Hause.   **R / F**

c In Deutschland kann man sitzen bleiben.   **R / F**

d In Großbritannien gehen Kinder mit vier Jahren zur Schule.   **R / F**

e In Deutschland muss man eine Uniform tragen.   **R / F**

f In Deutschland gehen Kinder mit sechs Jahren zur Schule.   **R / F**

g In Großbritannien macht man Abitur.   **R / F**

h Im Gymnasium macht man Gymnastik.   **R / F**

**2** 🎧 **Listen to these people and answer the questions.**

1 What is this boy doing? *an apprenticeship*

2 What is this girl doing next year? _____

3 What kind of school does this boy go to? _____

4 What kind of school does this girl go to? _____

5 Is this boy at university? _____

6 Is this girl doing the German equivalent of A-levels? _____

**3** **Read these sentences and put a tick if you agree with the opinion and a cross if you don't. Explain your answers, in English or German.**

a Der Unterricht beginnt um acht Uhr. Das ist super. ☐

b Man muss eine Uniform tragen. Das ist doof. ☐

c Man geht um ein Uhr nach Hause. Das ist zu früh. ☐

d Man kann sitzen bleiben. Das macht Spaß. ☐

e Die Kinder kommen mit vier Jahren zur Schule. Das ist zu jung. ☐

f Die Schüler essen in der Kantine. Das ist besser, als um elf Uhr ein Käsebrot zu essen. ☐

**1** *Schulfächerquiz.* Solve the clues and write the German words for the subjects into the grid. What is the mystery subject (in tinted box down)?

1 Tiere und Pflanzen

2 Länder

3 Klassik oder Pop

4 Die Sprache in Großbritannien

5 Die Sprache in Deutschland

6 Computerkunde

7 "Bonjour!"

8 Nicht Biologie, nicht Chemie …

9 Picasso, Magritte, Monet …

10 Zwei plus zwei ist vier

The mystery subject is: _____

**2** Read the email below and answer the questions in German.

**a** Wohnt Sonja in England? *Nein, sie wohnt in Deutschland.*

**b** Was ist Sonjas Lieblingsfach? _____

**c** Muss sie dieses Fach lernen? _____

**d** Seit wann lernt sie dieses Fach? _____

**e** Wie findet Sonja Physik? _____

**f** Was wird sie statt Physik lernen? _____

**g** Warum? _____

**h** Was wird sie an der Uni machen? _____

**Hallo Kate!**
Welche Fächer lernst du in deiner Schule in England? Mein Lieblingsfach ist Englisch. Bei uns in Deutschland ist das ein Pflichtfach. Ich lerne schon seit fünf Jahren Englisch.

Ich finde Physik nicht so toll. Ich finde dieses Fach langweilig und schwer. Ich werde Physik nach der elften Klasse aufgeben und stattdessen* Erdkunde machen. Dieses Jahr habe ich in Erdkunde sehr gute Noten bekommen und ich finde es sehr interessant, etwas über andere Länder zu lernen.

In zwei Jahren werde ich Abitur machen und dann werde ich hoffentlich an der Uni Geographie studieren.
Bis bald,
Sonja

*stattdessen – *instead*

# 4B.4 Berufe

**1** **Write in the words for these people's jobs.**

a Ich bin _Ärztin_____ .
(*female doctor*)

b Ich bin _____ .
(*housewife*)

c Ich bin _____ .
(*postman*)

d Ich bin _____ .
(*policewoman*)

e Ich bin _____ .
(*female nurse*)

f Ich bin _____ .
(*male lorry driver*)

g Ich bin _____ .
(*male computer programmer*)

h Ich bin _____ .
(*female secretary*)

**2** **Write in the jobs that these people would like to do, using the box below to help. Remember to adjust the word according to whether the person is male or female.**

a Petra: Ich will in einer Schule mit Kindern arbeiten.

Ich möchte _____ werden.

b Hans: Ich will zu Hause bleiben und die Hausarbeit machen.

Ich möchte _____ werden.

c Birgit: Ich möchte in einem Krankenhaus arbeiten.

Ich möchte _____ werden.

d Boris: Ich möchte Flugzeuge fliegen.

Ich möchte _____ werden.

e Iris: Ich will in einem Geschäft arbeiten.

Ich möchte _____ werden.

f Klaus: Wenn Leute krank sind, möchte ich helfen.

Ich möchte _____ werden.

g Claudia: Ich arbeite gern am Computer.

Ich möchte _____ werden.

> Informatiker/in
> Pilot/in
> Lehrer/in
> Krankenpfleger/in
> Arzt/Ärztin
> Verkäufer/in
> Hausfrau/mann

**1** 🎧 **Listen to Svenja and her mother and fill the gaps – just one word for each gap.**

**a** Heute war die Schule ___langweilig___ .

**b** Französisch war _____ und die Lehrerin war

_____ .

**c** Der Deutschlehrer war _____ .

**d** Frau Meyer ist _____ .

**e** Svenja ist fast _____ .

**f** Mathe hat keinen _____ gemacht.

**g** Die _____ war toll!

**h** Svenja hat _____ gegessen.

**2** **Remember that the verb always comes second in a German sentence. Put these sentences into German, using the beginnings provided.**

**a** *We had biology in the first lesson.*

Heute ___hatten wir Biologie in der ersten Stunde___ .

**b** *Children go to school at the age of six.*

In der Schweiz _____ .

**c** *We drink milk.*

In der Pause _____ .

**d** *The teaching is interesting.*

In meiner Schule _____ .

**e** *We will go to grammar school.*

Nächstes Jahr _____ .

**f** *Ursel went to primary school.*

Letztes Jahr _____ .

**g** *I'd like to become a teacher.*

Später _____ .

**h** *I will do homework.*

Am Wochenende _____ .

## 1 *für* + accusative
**What is this person saving for? Write in *einen* (m), *eine* (f) or *ein* (n).**

Ich spare für _____ein_____ Handy, _____ E-Gitarre, _____ Computer, _____ Rad, _____ MP3-player und _____ Uhr.

| masculine | feminine | neuter |
|-----------|----------|--------|
| Computer | Gitarre | Handy |
| MP3-Player | Uhr | Rad |

## 2 Present, perfect and future
**This person has changed her habits. Put each present tense sentence into the perfect and then the future, using the details given in brackets at the end.**

**a** *Present*: Normalerweise dusche ich um 6 Uhr.

*Perfect*: Gestern _habe ich um 7 Uhr geduscht._ (um 7 Uhr)

*Future*: Morgen _werde ich ..._ (um 8 Uhr)

**b** *Present*: Normalerweise esse ich Cornflakes zum Frühstück.

*Perfect*: Gestern _____ (Toast)

*Future*: Morgen _____ (Joghurt)

**c** *Present*: Normalerweise fahre ich mit dem Bus zur Schule.

*Perfect*: Gestern _____ (Auto)

*Future*: Morgen _____ (Rad)

> Remember, many verbs use *haben* to form the perfect tense, but some – including *fahren* – use *sein* instead.

**d** *Present*: Normalerweise fahren wir in den Ferien nach Frankreich.

*Perfect*: Letztes Jahr _____ (Spanien)

*Future*: Nächstes Jahr _____ (Schweden)

**e** *Present*: Normalerweise spiele ich am Wochenende Fußball.

*Perfect*: Letztes Wochenende _____ (Tennis)

*Future*: Nächstes Wochenende _____ (Volleyball)

**f** *Present*: Normalerweise mache ich meine Hausaufgaben um 15 Uhr.

*Perfect*: Gestern _____ (um 16 Uhr)

*Future*: Morgen _____ (gar nicht!)

## 'Filler' words

**1**  Read the message and cross out all the 'filler' words.

> Na, wie war denn die Party
> eigentlich? Also, ich fand sie
> ganz gut. Naja, die Musik
> war etwas altmodisch, aber
> das Essen war wirklich lecker.

- Note that when you have taken out all the unnecessary words, it is still completely understandable. We do the same in English, often using words such as 'well' and 'like'.

## Working out the meaning of unknown words

**2**  In German, words are put together to make new ones. Draw one line to match the German words to the English explanations and another line to the actual English meanings.

| Gesamtschule | flying thing | postman |
| Nachhilfe | hour plan | nurse |
| Nebenjob | stay sitting | confectionery |
| Süßigkeit | letter carrier | comprehensive school |
| Fahrrad | earth studies | bike |
| Zeitschrift | sweetness | tuition |
| Stundenplan | school yard | magazine |
| Oberstufe | carer of the sick | aeroplane |
| sitzen bleiben | after help | repeat a school year |
| Schulhof | upper stage | geography |
| Erdkunde | time writing | timetable |
| Krankenpflegerin | whole school | sixth form |
| Briefträger | side job | playground |
| Flugzeug | driving wheel | part-time job |

| Ich habe einen Nebenjob | *I have a part-time job* |
|---|---|
| Ich trage Zeitungen aus. | *I deliver newspapers.* |
| Ich mache Babysitting. | *I do babysitting.* |
| Ich führe Hunde aus. | *I walk dogs.* |
| Ich arbeite in einem Geschäft. | *I work in a shop.* |
| Ich helfe im Garten. | *I do gardening.* |
| Ich wasche Autos. | *I wash cars.* |
| Ich gebe Nachhilfeunterricht. | *I give extra tuition.* |
| Ich helfe zu Hause. | *I help at home.* |
| Ich bekomme kein Taschengeld. | *I don't get any pocket money.* |
| Ich bekomme 8 Euro pro Stunde. | *I get 8 euros an hour.* |
| Ich arbeite, um … zu kaufen. | *I work to buy …* |
| Ich spare für … | *I'm saving up for …* |
| ein Fahrrad/ ein Handy | *a bike/ a mobile phone* |
| Kleidung/Make-up. | *clothes/make-up.* |

| Meine Schule | *My school* |
|---|---|
| die Gesamtschule | *comprehensive school* |
| das Gymnasium | *grammar school* |
| die Hauptschule | *secondary school (to age 15)* |
| die Realschule | *secondary school (to age 16)* |
| die Grundshule | *primary school* |
| Ich besuche eine/die Gesamtschule. | *I go to a comprehensive school.* |
| Ich gehe auf ein/das Gymnasium. | *I go to a grammar school.* |
| Ich bin in der 10. Klasse. | *I'm in Year 11.* |
| Ich werde … | *I will …* |
| mein Abitur machen. | *do my A levels.* |
| eine Lehre machen. | *do an apprenticeship.* |
| auf die Oberstufe kommen. | *go into the sixth form.* |
| meinen Realschulabschluss machen. | *do my GCSEs.* |
| an der Universität studieren. | *study at university.* |

| Und nächstes Jahr? | *And next year?* |
|---|---|
| Biologie | *biology* |
| Chemie | *chemistry* |
| Chinesisch | *Chinese* |
| Deutsch | *German* |
| Englisch | *English* |
| Erdkunde | *geography* |
| Französisch | *French* |
| Geschichte | *history* |
| Informatik | *IT* |
| Kunst | *art* |
| Mathe | *maths* |
| Musik | *music* |
| Naturwissenschaften | *science* |
| Physik | *physics* |
| Religion | *religious education* |

| Spanisch | *Spanish* |
|---|---|
| Sport | *PE* |
| … ist mein Lieblingsfach. | *… is my favourite subject.* |
| Ich bekomme gute Noten. | *I get good grades.* |
| Ich habe … als Leistungskurs gewählt. | *I chose … as main/specialist subjects.* |
| Ich lerne seit zwei Jahren … | *I've been learning … for two years.* |

| Berufe | *Professions* |
|---|---|
| Ich möchte … werden. | *I'd like to be a …* |
| Arzt, Ärztin | *doctor* |
| Briefträger/in | *postman/woman* |
| Geschäftsmann, Geschäftsfrau | *businessman/woman* |
| Hausmann, Hausfrau | *house husband, housewife* |
| Informatiker/in | *IT specialist* |
| Kellner/in | *waiter, waitress* |
| Krankenpfleger/in | *nurse* |
| Lkw-Fahrer/in | *truck driver* |
| Modedesigner/in | *fashion designer* |
| Polizist/in | *policeman/woman* |
| Sekretär/in | *secretary* |
| Tierarzt, Tierärztin | *vet* |
| Verkäufer/in | *shop assistant* |

## Checklist

| How well do you think you can do the following? Write a sentence for each one if you can. | | | |
|---|---|---|---|
| | I can do this well | I can do this but not very well | I can't do this yet |
| 1. talk about part-time jobs, spending and saving | | | |
| 2. talk about school life in Germany / UK | | | |
| 3. talk about what I've done this year at school and what I'm going to do next year | | | |
| 4. talk about different jobs and say what job I would like to do in the future | | | |
| 5. use masculine and feminine forms of job words | | | |
| 6. use *ich möchte … werden* | | | |

# Zoom Deutsch 2 Higher Workbook CD Track listings

1    Copyright line

**Pronunciation**

2    Seite 4, Consonants/Konsonanten
3    Seite 4, *g*
4    Seite 4, *j*
5    Seite 4, *r*
6    Seite 4, *s; sp, st*
7    Seite 4, Übung 1
8    Seite 4, *ß*
9    Seite 5, *ss*
10   Seite 5, Übung 2
11   Seite 5, *v*
12   Seite 5, *w*
13   Seite 5, Übung 3
14   Seite 5, *z*
15   Seite 5, Combination of consonants *ch*
16   Seite 5, *ig*
17   Seite 5, *sch*
18   Seite 5, *pf*
19   Seite 5, *zw*
20   Seite 6, Vowels/Vokale long a/langes *a*
21   Seite 6, short *a*/ kurzes *a*
22   Seite 6, hat/ cat/ Handy
23   Seite 6, short *e*/ kurzes *e*
24   Seite 6, long *e*/ langes *e*
25   Seite 6, Übung 4
26   Seite 6, *i*
27   Seite 6, short *o*/kurzes *o*
28   Seite 6, long *o*/ langes *o*
29   Seite 6, Übung 5
30   Seite 7, *u*
31   Seite 7, long *u*/ langes *u*
32   Seite 7, Übung 6
33   Seite 7, Combination of vowels *ie*
34   Seite 7, *ei*
35   Seite 7, Übung 7
36   Seite 7, *au*
37   Seite 7, Umlauts *a ä*
38   Seite 7, *o ö*
39   Seite 7, *u ü*
40   Seite 7, Übung 8

**Einheit 0: Hallo!**

41   Seite 8, Übung 2
42   Seite 9, Übung 2
43   Seite 10, Übung 3
44   Seite 11, Übung 2
45   Seite 12, Übung 2

**Einheit 1A: Mein Tag**

46   Seite 17, Übungen 3 und 4
47   Seite 18, Übung 1
48   Seite 19, Übung 1
49   Seite 22, Übung 1

**Einheit 1B: Wir feiern!**

50   Seite 25, Übung 2
51   Seite 27, Übung 1

**Einheit 2A: Die Medien**

52   Seite 35, Übungen 1 und 2
53   Seite 36, Übung 2
54   Seite 38, Übung 1

**Einheit 2B: Hobbys**

55   Seite 40, Übung 3
56   Seite 42, Übung 3
57   Seite 43, Übung 1
58   Seite 46, Übung 1

**Einheit 3A: Gesundes Leben**

59   Seite 49, Übung 2
60   Seite 50, Übung 2
61   Seite 51, Übung 2

**Einheit 3B: Ausflug nach Düsseldorf**

62   Seite 57, Übung 1
63   Seite 58, Übungen 1 und 2
64   Seite 61, Übung 1

**Einheit 4A: Die Umwelt**

65   Seite 64, Übung 2
66   Seite 66, Übung 4
67   Seite 68, Übung 1

**Einheit 4B: Schule und Zukunft**

68   Seite 72, Übungen 2 und 3
69   Seite 73, Übung 2
70   Seite 76, Übung 1